The Mathematics of Saving
Mathematics for Everyday Living

Roland E. Larson

Robert P. Hostetler

Exercises prepared with the assistance of

David E. Heyd

Updated and revised by

Marjorie J. Bertram

meridian

CREATIVE GROUP

A DIVISION OF LARSON TEXTS, INC.

This book is published by
Meridian Creative Group, a Division of Larson Texts, Inc.

Please address all correspondence to:
Home School Division
Meridian Creative Group
5178 Station Road
Erie, PA 16510
(800) 695-9427
http://www.home.meridiancg.com

Trademark acknowledgement:
Explorer Plus is a trademark of Texas Instruments Incorporated

Printed in the United States of America

International Standard Book Number: ISBN 1-887050-24-8

10 9 8 7 6 5 4 3 2 1

Preface

Mathematics for Everyday Living is a series of workbooks designed to give students a solid and practical grasp of the mathematics used in daily life.

Each workbook in the series features practical consumer information, solved examples, and "Try one!" exercises with which students can use a particular skill immediately following its introduction. Complete solutions to the "Try one!" exercises are provided in the back of the workbook along with answers to odd-numbered exercises.

The workbook, *"The Mathematics of Saving,"* is divided into five sections, each of which address a set of mathematical skills and concepts that teach students ways in which to save their money.

- In the first section, "Simple Interest and Effective Yield," students will learn how to calculate simple interest. Also discussed is the annual effective yield and the way in which it can be used to compare different interest rates.

- In section two, "Compound Interest," students will learn how savings account balances can increase more quickly when interest is compounded.

- Section three, "Increasing Annuities," teaches students that money can quickly grow when deposited regularly in an increasing annuity. Also shown is how to calculate the resulting balance after repeated deposits.

- In section four, "Decreasing Annuities," students are taught how to determine the initial deposit necessary to withdraw regular amounts from an account. Certain exercises demonstrate the advantages of setting up a decreasing annuity that pays over time.

- Section five presents a spotlight on a career in banking. Several different types of banking careers are discussed along with their educational requirements. Included in this section is a comprehensive set of review exercises asked within the context of a career in banking.

Finally, a "Thank-you" is owed to Richard Bertram for his patience and support, John Spring and Bob Snyder for their technical assistance, and Cheryl Bernik for her help in organizing this project.

Marjorie J. Bertram

Contents

Section 1
Simple Interest and Effective Yield

Setting money aside for the future has never been easy; nevertheless, it has always been one of mankind's most hallowed virtues. There are many *reasons for saving money*: for the down payment on a house, college tuition, retirement, a vacation, a new stereo, a general sense of satisfaction, a rainy day, or for any number of other reasons. Not only are there many reasons for saving, there are almost as many *ways to save money*: passbook savings accounts, target savings plans, savings certificates, bonds, securities, payroll deduction plans, savings transfer checking accounts, time deposits, and many others.

The basic concept of saving is simple. A certain sum of money called the **principal** is deposited in an account and at a later time a larger **amount** (or **balance**) is withdrawn. The difference between the amount and principal is called the **interest**. These quantities are related in the following way.

P = Principal

A = Amount (or balance)

I = Interest

Amount = Principal + Interest

$A = P + I$

EXAMPLE 1	**Finding the interest given the principal and the amount**

Elaine Dwyer deposits $1000.00 in a new passbook savings account on July 10th, and at the end of the year her balance is $1026.57. Elaine is required to list the interest from this account on her income tax form for the year. How much interest should Elaine list from this account?

1

SOLUTION

Elaine's initial deposit is $1000.00, and we have

Principal = P = $1000.00.

The balance at the end of the year is

Amount = A = $1026.57.

Therefore, from the formula $A = P + I$, we have $I = A - P$ and thus,

Interest = $I = A - P$

$$= \$1026.57 - \$1000.00$$

$$= \$26.57.$$ ◆

Try one!

Marty Forbes deposits $2500.00 in a new passbook savings account on May 31st, and at the end of the year his balance is $2593.75. Marty is required to list the interest from this account on his income tax form for the year. How much interest should Marty list from this account?

Answer: _____

There are many ways in which savings institutions compute interest on savings accounts. The oldest (and easiest) is called the **simple interest** method. The formula for simple interest involves three quantities

P = Principal

R = Annual Percentage Rate

T = Time (interest period in years or parts of years)

Interest = (Principal)(Annual Percentage Rate)(Time)

$I = PRT.$

In practice, this method of computing interest is used for interest periods of *at most* one year ($T \leq 1$).

EXAMPLE 2   Finding the interest given the principal, rate, and time

Ron Brooks is a member of a church that is planning to build a new sanctuary. To raise money for the project, the church decides to sell bonds that pay 5% simple interest per year. Ron purchases $2500.00 worth of the bonds and is sent a check for the interest each year. What is the amount of Ron's yearly interest check?

SOLUTION

For this problem, we have P = $2500.00, R = 0.05, and T = 1. Thus, the interest for one year is

$I = PRT$

$= (\$2500.00)(0.05)(1)$

$= \$125.00.$ ◆

Try one!

Steve Jenkins is a member of Ron Brooks' church (see Example 2).
Steve purchased $1750.00 worth of the bonds at the same time Ron did.
What is the amount of Steve's yearly interest check?

Answer: _____

In Example 2, the interest period used in the formula $I = PRT$ is
one year ($T = 1$). When the interest period involves less than one
year, we represent the time as a fractional part of the year by divid-
ing the number of days by 365. (For **leap years**, divide by 366.)

D = interest period in days

$$T = \frac{D}{365}$$

One type of savings account is the *passbook* (or *regular savings*)
account. In this type of account, interest is usually figured on a
day-of-deposit to **day-of-withdrawal** basis with no penalty for
transfering money in and out of the account. Although policies vary
from one financial institution to another, it is not uncommon to find
passbook accounts which pay simple interest on deposits of ninety
days or less. (Actually, the more common practice with passbook
accounts is to compound the interest daily. We will look at this
method of computing interest in Section 2.)

EXAMPLE 3   **Finding the interest given the principal, rate, and days**

Marianne Troutman opens a passbook savings account and makes an initial deposit of $350.00. For periods of up to ninety days, this particular passbook account pays simple interest at the rate of $3\frac{1}{4}\%$ per year. If Marianne makes no other deposits, find the interest and the balance for the following periods of time. (Assume a non leap year.)

a. 1 day   **b.** 30 days   **c.** 90 days

SOLUTION

In each of the three cases, we have $P = \$350.00$ and $R = 0.0325$.

a. If $D = 1$, we have

$$I = PRT = PR\left(\frac{D}{365}\right)$$

$$= (\$350.00)(0.0325)\left(\frac{1}{365}\right)$$

$$\approx \$0.03,$$

and the balance after one day is

$$A = P + I$$

$$= \$350.00 + \$0.03$$

$$= \$350.03.$$

b. If $D = 30$, we have

$$I = PRT = PR\left(\frac{D}{365}\right)$$

$$= (\$350.00)(0.0325)\left(\frac{30}{365}\right)$$

$$\approx \$0.93,$$

and the balance after thirty days is

$$A = P + I$$

$$= \$350.00 + \$0.93$$

$$= \$350.93.$$

c. If $D = 90$, we have

$$I = PRT = PR\left(\frac{D}{365}\right)$$

$$= (\$350.00)(0.0325)\left(\frac{90}{365}\right)$$

$$\approx \$2.80,$$

and the balance after ninety days is

$$A = P + I$$

$$= \$350.00 + \$2.80$$

$$= \$352.80.$$ ◆

Try one!

Marianne Troutman opens a different type of passbook savings account and makes an initial deposit of \$750.00. For periods of up to 180 days, this particular passbook account pays simple interest at the rate of $4\frac{1}{4}\%$ per year. If Marianne makes no other deposits, find the interest and the balance for 175 days. (Assume a non leap year.)

Interest: _____ Balance: _____

The method of computing the number of days between a savings deposit and a withdrawal may vary slightly from one institution to another. Some institutions figure the day-of-deposit and the day-of-withdrawal to be the actual days on which the transaction takes place. Others consider the day-of-deposit and the day-of-withdrawal to be the days on which the transactions are posted in the account. The posting date may or may not correspond with the transaction date. For example, many institutions do not post late afternoon transactions until the next working day.

EXAMPLE 4   Finding the day-of-deposit

Bill Kelley deposited the following amounts into his savings account in October:

a. $100.00 at 10:00 a.m. on Monday, October 5.

b. $100.00 at 4:00 p.m. on Thursday, October 8.

c. $50.00 at 4:00 p.m. on Friday, October 9.

Find the day-of-deposit for each of Bill's deposits if the posting policy at Bill's bank is that all transactions before 3:00 p.m. are posted the same day and all transactions after 3:00 p.m. are posted the next *business* day.

SOLUTION

a. This deposit was made before 3:00 p.m. and was posted the same day. Thus, the day-of-deposit was October 5.

b. This deposit was made after 3:00 p.m. on Thursday and was not posted until Friday. Thus, the day-of-deposit was October 9.

c. This deposit was made after 3:00 p.m. on Friday and was not posted until the next working day. Since Monday, October 12, was Columbus Day, the day-of-deposit was October 13.   ◆

Try one!

Find the day-of-deposit for a deposit of $200.00 on Friday, December 22 at 4:00 p.m. if the posting policy at a particular bank is that all transactions before 3:00 p.m. are posted the same day and all transactions after 3:00 p.m. are posted the next *working* day.

Answer: _____

Interest in a day-of-deposit to day-of-withdrawal savings account is figured from the day-of-deposit *up to, but not including the day-of-withdrawal*. For example, if the day-of-deposit is March 4 and the day-of-withdrawal is March 27 (that same month), the number of days the deposit earned interest is

$$D = 27 - 4 = 23 \text{ days.}$$

That is, interest is computed from the 4th through the 26th, but not the 27th. (See Table 1.)

TABLE 1   **March***

		Day-of-Deposit: March 4				**Day-of-Withdrawal: March 27**	
S	**M**	**T**	**W**	**T**	**F**	**S**	**Number of Days**
1	2	3	4	5	6	7	4
8	9	10	11	12	13	14	7
15	16	17	18	19	20	21	7
22	23	24	25	26	27	28	5
29	30	31					–
							Total = 23 days

*Interest earning days are underlined.

For time periods extending over two or more months, it is convenient to assign a number to each day of the year as shown in Table 2. Using this table, we can find the number of days from *day n* up to but not including *day m* as follows.

Time period begins and ends in same calendar year:

$$D = m - n$$

Time period involves two calendar years (*m* and *n* are in consecutive years):

$$D = 365^* + m - n$$

*366 if period begins before February 29 in a leap year.

TABLE 2   **Number of Each Day in the Year**

Day of Month	Jan.	Feb.	Mar.	Apr.	May	June	July	Aug.	Sept.	Oct.	Nov.	Dec	Day of Month
1	1	32	60	91	121	152	182	213	244	274	305	335	1
2	2	33	61	92	122	153	183	214	245	275	306	336	2
3	3	34	62	93	123	154	184	215	246	276	307	337	3
4	4	35	63	94	124	155	185	216	247	277	308	338	4
5	5	36	64	95	125	156	186	217	248	278	309	339	5
6	6	37	65	96	126	157	187	218	249	279	310	340	6
7	7	38	66	97	127	158	188	219	250	280	311	341	7
8	8	39	67	98	128	159	189	220	251	281	312	342	8
9	9	40	68	99	129	160	190	221	252	282	313	343	9
10	10	41	69	100	130	161	191	222	253	283	314	344	10
11	11	42	70	101	131	162	192	223	254	284	315	345	11
12	12	43	71	102	132	163	193	224	255	285	316	346	12
13	13	44	72	103	133	164	194	225	256	286	317	347	13
14	14	45	73	104	134	165	195	226	257	287	318	348	14
15	15	46	74	105	135	166	196	227	258	288	319	349	15
16	16	47	75	106	136	167	197	228	259	289	320	350	16
17	17	48	76	107	137	168	198	229	260	290	321	351	17
18	18	49	77	108	138	169	199	230	261	291	322	352	18
19	19	50	78	109	139	170	200	231	262	292	323	353	19
20	20	51	79	110	140	171	201	232	263	293	324	354	20
21	21	52	80	111	141	172	202	233	264	294	325	355	21
22	22	53	81	112	142	173	203	234	265	295	326	356	22
23	23	54	82	113	143	174	204	235	266	296	327	357	23
24	24	55	83	114	144	175	205	236	267	297	328	358	24
25	25	56	84	115	145	176	206	237	268	298	329	359	25
26	26	57	85	116	146	177	207	238	269	299	330	360	26
27	27	58	86	117	147	178	208	239	270	300	331	361	27
28	28	59	87	118	148	179	209	240	271	301	332	362	28
29	29	*	88	119	149	180	210	241	272	302	333	363	29
30	30	–	89	120	150	181	211	242	273	303	334	364	30
31	31	–	90	–	151	–	212	243	–	304	–	365	31

*On leap year, February 29 is day 60 and the number of each day after February 29 is increased by one.

Remember that years that are divisible by four are leap years (1992, 1996, 2000, etc.).

> ### EXAMPLE 5   Finding the number of days in a time period

Find the number of interest earning days for the following deposits.

Day-of-Deposit	Day-of-Withdrawal
a. January 29, 1991	September 4, 1991
b. January 29, 1992	September 4, 1992

SOLUTION

a. Since January 29, 1991 is day 29, $n = 29$. September 4, 1991 is day 247; therefore, $m = 247$. Using the formula $D = m - n$, we have $D = m - n = 247 - 29 = 218$ days.

b. Since January 29, 1992 is day 29, $n = 29$. However, since 1992 is a leap year, September 4, 1992 is day 248. Therefore, $m = 248$. So we have $D = m - n = 248 - 29 = 219$ days. ◆

Try one!

Find the number of interest earning days for the following deposits.

Day-of-Deposit	Day-of-Withdrawal
a. August 27, 1995	December 16, 1995

Answer: _____

Day-of-Deposit	Day-of-Withdrawal
b. February 11, 1996	January 7, 1997

Answer: _____

If we know the *simple* interest I, the principal P, and the time T, then the **annual percentage rate** R can be determined as follows:

$$\text{Annual Percentage Rate} = \frac{\text{Interest}}{(\text{Principal})(\text{Time})}$$

$$R = \frac{I}{PT} = \frac{I}{P\left(\frac{D}{365}\right)}.$$

Calculator Hints

$$R = \frac{I}{PT} = \frac{I}{P\left(\frac{D}{365}\right)}$$

To find R for simple interest using your calculator, apply the following steps:

1. Divide D by 365.

2. Multiply by P.

3. Press $\boxed{1/X}$ and multiply by I.

4. Convert to percent by multiplying by 100.

EXAMPLE 6 — Finding the annual percentage rate for simple interest

Find the annual percentage rate for a principal of $175.00 yielding a simple interest of 77¢ in 60 days.

SOLUTION

Since $P = \$175.00$, $I = \$0.77$, and $D = 60$, we have

$$R = \frac{I}{P\left(\frac{D}{365}\right)} = \frac{\$0.77}{(\$175.00)\left(\frac{60}{365}\right)} \approx 0.02677 \approx 2.68\%. \quad \blacklozenge$$

EXAMPLE 6

Steps	Display
60 ÷ 365 =	0.164383562
× 175 =	28.76712329
1/x × 0.77 =	0.026766667
× 100 =	2.676666667

EXAMPLE 7 — Finding the annual percentage rate for simple interest

Find the annual percentage rate for a principal of $10,000.00 increasing by simple interest to a balance of $10,356.79 in 345 days.

SOLUTION

Since $A = \$10,365.79$ and $P = \$10,000.00$, we have

$$I = A - P = \$10,365.79 - \$10,000.00 = \$365.79.$$

Furthermore, since $D = 345$,

$$R = \frac{I}{P\left(\frac{D}{365}\right)} = \frac{\$365.79}{(\$10,000.00)\left(\frac{345}{365}\right)} \approx 0.03870 = 3.87\%. \quad \blacklozenge$$

EXAMPLE 8   **Finding the annual percentage rate for simple interest**

Find the annual percentage rate for a deposit of $450.00 on March 11, 1995 that was withdrawn along with simple interest of $8.11 on October 28, 1995.

SOLUTION

From March 11, 1995 to October 28, 1995 we have (by Table 2)

$$D = m - n = 301 - 70 = 231.$$

Since $P = \$450.00$ and $I = \$8.11$, we have

$$R = \frac{I}{P\left(\frac{D}{365}\right)} = \frac{\$8.11}{(\$450.00)\left(\frac{231}{365}\right)} \approx 0.02848 \approx 2.85\%. \qquad \blacklozenge$$

Try one!

Find the annual percentage rate for a deposit of $968.50 on January 19, 1996 that was withdrawn along with simple interest of $28.39 on December 2, 1996. (Note: 1996 was a leap year.)

Answer: _____

The simple interest method is only one of numerous existing methods of calculating interest. (We will look at other common methods in Section 2.) Along with its primary use in calculating interest, the simple interest method has an important secondary use–providing a "yardstick" by which we can compare different interest rates. To construct this yardstick, we begin with the annual percentage rate for simple interest

$$R = \frac{I}{PT}$$

and let $T = 1$. Now, for this special case in which the time period is precisely *one year*, we define the ratio of the interest to the principal to be the **annual effective yield** (or annual effective rate).

$$\text{Annual Effective Yield} = \frac{\text{Interest (for one year)}}{\text{Principal (at beginning of year)}}$$

$$Y = \frac{I}{P}$$

EXAMPLE 9   Finding the annual effective yield

Richard and Jeannie Muller have two different savings plans that accumulated the following amounts of interest *during the year* from January 1, 1996 to January 1, 1997.

a. A passbook savings account that accumulated $24.03 in interest on a beginning principal of $850.00.

b. A certificate of deposit that accumulated $20.79 in interest on a beginning principal of $500.00.

Which of these two accounts paid the higher annual effective yield?

SOLUTION

Note that to find the annual effective yield it is not necessary to know the method in which the interest in each account was computed.

a. For the passbook savings account, the annual effective yield is

$$Y = \frac{I}{P} = \frac{\$24.03}{\$850.00} \approx 0.02827 \approx 2.83\%.$$

b. For the certificate of deposit, the annual effective yield is

$$Y = \frac{I}{P} = \frac{\$20.79}{\$500.00} = 0.04158 \approx 4.16\%.$$

Of the two savings plans, the certificate of deposit paid the higher yield.   ◆

Try one!

Richard and Jeannie Muller (from Example 9) had one additional savings plan called a tax-exempt municipal bond. Determine the annual effective yield in the year from January 1, 1996 to January 1, 1997 for this tax-exempt municipal bond if it accumulated $75.00 in interest on a beginning principal of $2500.00.

Answer: _____

The interest earned in most types of savings accounts is taxable. This is true of interest earned on savings accounts in banks, savings and loan associations, and credit unions. However, certain types of governmental savings plans, such as municipal bonds, yield tax-free interest. Whether interest is taxed or not can make quite a difference in the actual yield on a savings account. For instance, in the previous example and its corresponding "Try-one!," if Richard and Jeannie are in an income tax bracket of 33% (including federal, state, and local income taxes) they would have had to pay $7.93 income tax on their interest of $24.03, and $6.86 income tax on their interest of $20.79. Taking this into account, Richard and Jeannie's annual effective yield *after taxes* is

For the passbook savings: $\dfrac{\$24.03 - \$7.93}{\$850.00} \approx 1.89\%$

For the certificate of deposit: $\dfrac{\$20.79 - \$6.86}{\$500.00} \approx 2.79\%$

For the tax-free municipal bond: $\dfrac{\$75.00 - \$0.00^{*}}{\$2500.00} = 3.00\%$

*Since the municipal bond is tax-free, nothing is subtracted.

Since taxes can eat away significant portions of interest, the best comparison of interest rates is the **annual effective yield after taxes**. Using this comparison, Richard and Jeannie's highest yield actually came from the tax-free municipal bond. Of course, the yield after taxes depends upon the tax bracket of the person earning the interest. For the person whose **tax bracket** is *b,* the annual effective yield after taxes for one year's interest of *I* on a principal of *P* is

$$\text{Annual Effective Yield After Taxes} = Y^* = \frac{I - bI}{P} = \frac{I(1 - b)}{P}.$$

EXAMPLE 10   Finding the annual effective yield after taxes

Linda and Curt Anderson purchase (jointly, in their own names) a $1000.00 savings certificate each year for their daughter Anne's college tuition. The yearly interest is $54.78 per $1000.00 worth of certificates. If Linda and Curt are in a 35% tax bracket, what is the annual effective yield after taxes for these certificates?

SOLUTION

For a 35% tax bracket, we have $b = 0.35$ and

$$Y^* = \frac{I(1-b)}{P} = \frac{(\$54.78)(1-0.35)}{\$1000.00} \approx 3.56\%. \qquad \blacklozenge$$

EXAMPLE 3

Steps	Display
1 ⊟ 0.35 ⊜	0.65
⊠ 54.78 ⊜	35.607
÷ 1000 ⊜	0.035607

EXAMPLE 11   Finding the annual effective yield after taxes

If Linda and Curt (from Example 10) would purchase the certificates in Anne's name (listing themselves as custodians) the interest would be credited as income under Anne's social security number instead of their own. Assuming that Anne's income is too low to be taxed, what is the annual effective yield after taxes?

SOLUTION

For a 0% tax bracket, we have

$$Y^* = \frac{I(1-b)}{P} = \frac{(\$54.78)(1-0)}{\$1000.00} \approx 5.48\%. \qquad \blacklozenge$$

Try one!

Rob Taylor is in a 30% tax bracket. Find the annual effective yield after taxes for Rob's $2000.00 savings certificate that earned $75.00 in one year.

Answer: _____

Over long periods of time, seemingly small differences in effective yields can result in substantial differences in the actual amount saved. For example, if Linda and Curt (from Examples 10 and 11) continued to save $1000.00 (at 5.48% annual effective yield) every year for 17 years all the while leaving the interest in the account, at the end of the 17th year the account would amount to $28,420.30. Since $11,420.30 of this represents accumulated interest, Linda and Curt would have paid approximately $3997.11 (35% of $11,420.30) in extra income taxes over the seventeen years *if they had not listed the account in their daughter's name*. We will examine this type of savings (many equal deposits over a long period of time) more closely in Section 3.

Important Terms

A, amount; b, income tax bracket; P, principal; I, interest; T, time

leap year; day-of-deposit; day-of-withdrawal

D, number of days in interest period

n, m, number of day in year

R, annual percentage rate

Y, annual effective yield

Y^*, annual effective yield after taxes

Important Formulas

$$A = P + I \qquad\qquad I = PRT \qquad\qquad T = \frac{D}{365}$$

$$I = A - P \qquad\qquad R = \frac{I}{PT} \qquad\qquad R = \frac{I}{PT}$$

$$D = 365 + m - n \text{ for non leap years}$$

$$D = 366 + m - n \text{ for leap years}$$

$$\text{For } T = 1,\ Y = \frac{I}{P} \qquad\qquad \text{For } T = 1,\ Y^* = \frac{I(1 - b)}{P}$$

CONSUMER HINTS

- Saving money requires determination and careful planning. The six basic factors in any savings plan are:

  1. *Present assets (past income)* **2.** *Present debts (past expenses)*

  3. *Present income* **4.** *Present expenses*

  5. *Future income* **6.** *Future goals and expenses*

  A workable savings plan requires a careful accounting of these six categories. Ask yourself the question "Are the first five categories consistent with the sixth?"

- The best type of savings account depends upon:

  1. *The size of the deposit*–Larger deposits are usually able to command higher interest rates.

  2. *The length of the deposit*–Deposits left for longer times are usually able to collect higher rates. Be careful, though, if you contract for a long term and withdraw early, since you may be subject to a penalty.

  3. *Your own tax bracket*–The higher your bracket, the more advantage you can get from tax-free interest plans.

- If you are saving for someone else, such as your child, and your child's tax bracket is lower than yours, you can increase the effective yield by putting the savings account in your child's name.

- Remember that the best way to compare various interest rates is by the annual effective yield *after* taxes.

- If you are seeking professional advice in creating your savings plan, ask someone who has nothing to gain by steering you in a certain direction. Bankers, credit union officers, insurance sales representatives, savings and loan officers, stockbrokers, and realtors all have their own biases, which hinder them from giving objective advice.

SECTION 1 EXERCISES

1. Find the interest earned in the following savings accounts. (Assume there were no deposits or withdrawals during the year.)

    a. *Balance at beginning of year:*   *Balance at end of year:*
            $547.12 $562.59

    Answer: _____

    b. *Balance at beginning of year:*   *Balance at end of year:*
            $1250.00 $1302.06

    Answer: _____

    c. *Balance at beginning of year:*   *Balance at end of year:*
            $8742.15 $9169.86

    Answer: _____

2. Find the balance in the following savings accounts at the end of the year. (Assume there were no deposits or withdrawals during the year.)

    a. *Balance at beginning of year:*   *Interest earned during year:*
            $36.58 $1.97

    Answer: _____

    b. *Balance at beginning of year:*   *Interest earned during year:*
            $1557.25 $51.81

    Answer: _____

3. Find the interest earned in the following passbook savings accounts. (Assume there were no withdrawals during the year.)

	Balance at Beginning of Year	Deposits During Year	Balance at End of Year
a.	$378.56	$150.00 $250.00	$796.85

Answer: _____

	Balance at Beginning of Year	Deposits During Year	Balance at End of Year
b.	$874.06	$525.00 $400.00	$1852.15

Answer: _____

	Balance at Beginning of Year	Deposits During Year	Balance at End of Year
c.	$764.36	$210.00 $375.00 $280.00	$1653.23

Answer: _____

4. Find the balance in the following savings accounts at the end of the year. (Assume there were no withdrawals during the year.)

a.

Balance at Beginning of Year	Deposits During Year	Interest Earned During Year
$174.68	$750.00	$31.03

Answer: _____

b.

Balance at Beginning of Year	Deposits During Year	Interest Earned During Year
$58.16	$1200.00 $550.00	$42.77

Answer: _____

c.

Balance at Beginning of Year	Deposits During Year	Interest Earned During Year
$974.01	$400.00 $825.00	$68.94

Answer: _____

5. Find the simple interest on a deposit of $100.00 for 180 days at 5%. (Assume a non leap year.)

Answer: _____

6. Find the simple interest on a deposit of $500.00 for 120 days at 3%. (Assume a non leap year.)

Answer: _____

7. Find the simple interest on a deposit of $700.00 for 90 days at 2.75%. (Assume a non leap year.)

Answer: _____

8. Find the simple interest on a deposit of $1000.00 for 30 days at $7\frac{1}{2}$%. (Assume a non leap year.)

Answer: _____

9. Find the simple interest on a deposit of $250.00 for 283 days at 15%. (Assume a non leap year.)

Answer: _____

10. Find the simple interest on a deposit of $1500.00 for 100 days at $4\frac{3}{4}$%. (Assume a non leap year.)

Answer: _____

11. Find the simple interest on a deposit of $1000.00 for 45 days at 6%. (Assume a non leap year.)

Answer: _____

12. Find the simple interest on a deposit of $1640.00 for 75 days at 2.85%. (Assume a non leap year.)

Answer: _____

13. Find the simple interest on a deposit of $100.00 for 180 days at 5%. (Assume a leap year.)

Answer: _____

14. Find the simple interest on a deposit of $500.00 for 120 days at 3%. (Assume a leap year.)

Answer: _____

15. Find the simple interest on a deposit of $700.00 for 90 days at 2.75%. (Assume a leap year.)

Answer: _____

16. Find the simple interest on a deposit of $1000.00 for 30 days at $7\frac{1}{2}$%. (Assume a leap year.)

Answer: _____

17. Find the simple interest on a deposit of $250.00 for 283 days at 15%. (Assume a leap year.)

Answer: _____

18. Find the simple interest on a deposit of \$1500.00 for 100 days at $4\frac{3}{4}\%$. (Assume a leap year.)

Answer: _____

19. Find the simple interest on a deposit of \$1000.00 for 45 days at 6%. (Assume a leap year.)

Answer: _____

20. Find the number of days in the interest period from February 17, 1995 to June 10, 1995.

Answer: _____

21. Find the number of days in the interest period from May 24, 1992 to July 3, 1992.

Answer: _____

22. Find the number of days in the interest period from January 10, 1984 to March 10, 1984.

Answer: _____

23. Find the number of days in the interest period from November 28, 1993 to February 2, 1994.

Answer: _____

24. Find the simple interest on $250.00 from March 10, 1995 to September 6, 1995 at 18%.

Answer: _____

25. Find the simple interest on $1000.00 from November 30, 1991 to January 20, 1992 at $3\frac{1}{2}$%.

Answer: _____

26. Find the simple interest on $1500.00 from December 1, 1996 to February 1, 1997 at 4%.

Answer: _____

27. Find the simple interest on $200.00 from July 31, 1981 to October 25, 1981 at $11\frac{1}{2}$%.

Answer: _____

28. Find the simple interest on $250.00 from September 1, 1990 to February 1, 1991 at $4\frac{1}{4}\%$.

Answer: _____

29. Find the annual percentage rate for $75.00 *simple* interest on $1200.00 for one year. Round your answer to the nearest hundredth of a percent and assume it is a non leap year.

Answer: _____

30. Find the annual percentage rate for $7.40 *simple* interest on $500.00 for 180 days. Round your answer to the nearest hundredth of a percent and assume it is a non leap year.

Answer: _____

31. Find the annual percentage rate for $11.56 *simple* interest on $1250.00 for 90 days. Round your answer to the nearest hundredth of a percent and assume it is a non leap year.

Answer: _____

32. Find the annual percentage rate for $25.34 *simple* interest on $10,000.00 for 30 days. Round your answer to the nearest hundredth of a percent and assume it is a non leap year.

Answer: _____

33. Find the annual percentage rate for $75.00 *simple* interest on $1200.00 for one year. Round your answer to the nearest hundredth of a percent and assume it is a leap year.

Answer: _____

34. Find the annual percentage rate for $7.40 *simple* interest on $500.00 for 180 days. Round your answer to the nearest hundredth of a percent and assume it is a leap year.

Answer: _____

35. Find the annual percentage rate for $11.56 *simple* interest on $1250.00 for 90 days. Round your answer to the nearest hundredth of a percent and assume it is a leap year.

Answer: _____

36. Find the annual percentage rate for $25.34 *simple* interest on $10,000.00 for 30 days. Round your answer to the nearest hundredth of a percent and assume it is a leap year.

Answer: _____

37. Find the annual effective yield for a savings account that accumulated $110.00 interest on $2500.00. Assume that the interest period is one year.

Answer: _____

38. Find the annual effective yield for a certificate of deposit that accumulated $118.98 interest on $1900.00. Assume that the interest period is one year.

Answer: _____

39. Find the annual effective yield for a treasury note that accumulated $94.16 interest on $2000.00. Assume that the interest period is one year.

Answer: _____

40. Find the annual effective yield for a municipal bond that accumulated $33.58 interest on $1000.00. Assume that the interest period is one year.

Answer: _____

41. Find the annual effective yield *after taxes* for the savings plan in Exercise 37. Assume that the interest is being earned by a person in a 30% tax bracket and that this plan *is not* tax-exempt.

Answer: _____

42. Find the annual effective yield *after taxes* for the savings plan in Exercise 38. Assume that the interest is being earned by a person in a 30% tax bracket and that this plan *is not* tax-exempt.

Answer: _____

43. Find the annual effective yield *after taxes* for the savings plan in Exercise 39. Assume that the interest is being earned by a person in a 30% tax bracket and that this plan *is not* tax-exempt.

Answer: _____

44. A farmer can buy a new piece of equipment for $4500.00 now. If he waits another 10 months (300 days), the price is expected to increase to $4750.00. If the farmer can invest the $4500.00 now and earn $5\frac{3}{4}\%$ simple interest for 300 days, should he buy now or wait? How much will he save by adopting the better plan?

Buy now or wait? _____ Amount saved: _____

45. The formula $A = P + PRT = P(1 + RT)$ can be solved for P to yield the formula

$$P = \frac{A}{1 + RT} = \frac{A}{[1 + R(\frac{D}{365})]} .$$

Use this formula in parts **a** and **b** to find the principal required to produce the given amount.

a. Betty Roth needs $1000.00 in 90 days. If her money earns $5\frac{1}{2}\%$ simple interest, how much should she invest now so that the amount after 90 days will be $1000.00? (Assume it is not a leap year.)

Answer: _____

b. How much should be invested at $3\frac{3}{4}\%$ simple interest so that the balance after one year is $6000.00?

Answer: _____

Section 2
Compound Interest

Simple interest, as discussed in Section 1, is by definition based only on the initial deposit (the principal), which remains fixed during the entire interest period. A second method of computing interest involves **compound interest**. With this method, earned interest is periodically added to the principal. Each time interest is added to the principal, the interest is said to be *compounded*. The result of compounding interest is that starting with the second compounding, the account earns *interest on interest* in addition to earning interest on the principal.

Compound interest rates are always given as annual percentages, no matter how many times the interest is compounded per year. The most common compounding periods are

Annually	Once per year, $T = 1$
Quarterly	Four times per year, $T = \frac{1}{4}$
Monthly	Twelve times per year, $T = \frac{1}{12}$
Daily	365 times per year, $T = \frac{1}{365}$

EXAMPLE 1   Constructing a table for compound interest

Ray Patton deposits $1000.00 in a four-year savings certificate account which pays an annual rate of $3\frac{1}{4}\%$ compounded quarterly. Find the balance in Ray's account after one year.

SOLUTION

For the first quarter, we have $P = \$1000.00$, $R = 0.0325$, and $T = \frac{1}{4} = 0.25$. Thus, the interest at the end of one quarter is

$$I = PRT = (\$1000.00)(0.0325)(0.25) \approx \$8.13.$$

By adding this interest to Ray's principal, the *new principal* is

$$P = \$1000.00 \ + \ \$8.13 \ = \$1008.13$$

which means that the interest for the second quarter is

$$I = PRT = (\$1008.13)(0.0325)(0.25) \approx \$8.19.$$

Continuing this process, we have the results shown in Table 3.

| TABLE 3 | $1000.00 AT $3\frac{1}{4}$% INTEREST COMPOUNDED QUARTERLY | | |

Quarter	Principal	Interest	Balance
1	$1000.00	$8.13	$1008.13
2	$1008.13	$8.19	$1016.32
3	$1016.32	$8.26	$1024.58
4	$1024.58	$8.32	$1032.90

Thus, the balance at the end of one year is $1032.90.   ◆

Try one!

If Susan Ryan deposits $1575.00 in a four-year savings certificate account which pays an annual rate of 3.5% compounded quarterly, find the balance in her account after one year.

Answer: _____

EXAMPLE 2   **Finding the annual effective yield**

Find the annual effective yield for Ray Patton's savings certificate.
(See Example 1.)

SOLUTION

Since the interest on Ray's beginning principal of $1000.00 amount-
ed to $32.90 at the end of one year, the annual effective yield is

$$Y = \frac{I}{P} = \frac{\$32.90}{\$1000.00} = 0.0329 = 3.29\%.$$ ◆

Try one!

If Kenneth Moore deposited $2500.00 in a two-year savings certificate
account which pays an annual rate of $3\frac{3}{4}\%$ compounded every six
months, find the balance in his account after one year, what is the annual
effective yield for this account?

Balance: _____

Effective Yield: _____

Note in Examples 1 and 2 that if Ray had earned $3\frac{1}{4}\%$ *simple interest* on the $1000.00 for a year he would have had a balance of $1032.50 rather than $1032.90. Thus, Ray gained $0.40 in interest by quarterly compounding. This example shows an important difference between simple and compound interest: *The annual effective yield for simple interest is always the same as the annual percentage rate, whereas the annual effective yield for compound interest may be higher than the annual percentage rate.* For this reason, the annual percentage rate for compound interest is sometimes referred to as the **nominal rate**, implying that the effective rate is higher. The greater the number of compoundings per year, the larger the annual effective yield. For example, if Ray's account in Examples 1 and 2 had been compounded *monthly*, he would have the balance shown in Table 4 and his annual effective yield would have been 3.30%.

TABLE 4 $1000.00 AT $3\frac{1}{4}\%$ INTEREST COMPOUNDED MONTHLY

Month	Principal	Interest	Balance
1	$1000.00	$2.71	$1002.71
2	$1002.71	$2.72	$1005.43
3	$1005.43	$2.72	$1008.15
4	$1008.15	$2.73	$1010.88
5	$1010.88	$2.74	$1013.62
6	$1013.62	$2.75	$1016.37
7	$1016.37	$2.75	$1019.12
8	$1019.12	$2.76	$1021.88
9	$1021.88	$2.77	$1024.65
10	$1024.65	$2.78	$1027.43
11	$1027.43	$2.78	$1030.21
12	$1030.21	$2.79	$1033.00

As demonstrated by Table 4, increasing the number of compoundings per year not only increases the amount of the balance at the end of the year, it also increases the amount of *effort* required to find the balance. Fortunately, we can avoid this step-by-step procedure with the following formula for compound interest.

n = number of compoundings per year

N = *total* number of compoundings

Balance after N compoundings = $A = P\left(1 + \dfrac{R}{n}\right)^N$

For the four most common compounding periods, the formulas for compound interest are:

Calculator Hints

$A = P\left(1 + \dfrac{R}{n}\right)^N$

To find the amount of compound interest using your calculator, apply the following steps:

1. Divide R by n and add 1.

2. Raise to the Nth power.

3. Multiply by P.

4. Round to the nearest cent.

Annually

A = Amount or Balance

$A = P(1 + R)^N$

Quarterly

$P\left(1 + \dfrac{R}{4}\right)^N$

Monthly

$P\left(1 + \dfrac{R}{12}\right)^N$

Daily

$P\left(1 + \dfrac{R}{365}\right)^N$

EXAMPLE 3   Finding compound interest by formula

Suppose that Ray Patton's deposit (see Examples 1 and 2) of $1000.00 at $3\frac{1}{4}\%$ is compounded daily.

a. What is Ray's balance at the end of one year?

b. What is Ray's balance at the end of four years?

c. What is the annual effective yield for this account?

SOLUTION

a. Since $P = \$1000.00$ and $R = 0.0325$, we have a balance at the end of one year ($N = 365$ for daily compounding) of

$$A = P\left(1 + \frac{R}{365}\right)^N = (\$1000.00)\left(1 + \frac{0.0325}{365}\right)^{365} \approx \$1033.03.$$

EXAMPLE 3a

Steps	Display
0.0325 ÷ 365 =	0.000089041
+ 1 =	1.000089041
y^x 365 =	1.0330324
× 1000 =	1033.0324

b. At the end of *four* years, we would have

$$N = (4)(365) = 1460,$$

and the balance would be

$$A = P\left(1 + \frac{R}{365}\right)^N = (\$1000.00)\left(1 + \frac{0.0325}{365}\right)^{1460} \approx \$1138.82.$$

c. To find the annual effective yield for this account, we note that the interest after one year is

$$I = A - P = \$1033.03 - \$1000.00 = \$33.03.$$

Therefore, the annual effective yield is

$$Y = \frac{I}{P} = \frac{\$33.03}{\$1000.00} \approx 0.0330 = 3.30\%. \qquad \blacklozenge$$

Try one!

Andrew Winstead deposited $1500.00 in a four-year certificate of deposit at $4\frac{1}{4}\%$ compounded daily. Find Andrew's balance **a)** at the end of one year, **b)** at the end of four years, and **c)** find the annual effective yield for this account.

One Year: _____

Four Years: _____

Annual Effective Yield: _____

We should point out that the four formulas for compound interest do not always yield exactly the same balance as the step-by-step method since the step-by-step method may involve a round-off error. Furthermore, other differences may arise because some accounting procedures incorporate leap years and some do not, some compute quarters by the actual number of days in the quarter (90, 91, 92) rather than one fourth of a year, and so on. The point is that the formulas presented in this section may yield balances which differ by a few cents from those obtained by any given savings institution. As an example, the balance after daily compounding for one 91-day quarter in a leap year, with $P = \$1000.00$ and $R = 7\% = 0.07$ can be computed by either one of the following formulas.

$$A = (\$1000.00)\left(1 + \frac{0.07}{366}\right)^{91} = \$1017.56$$

$$A = (\$1000.00)\left(1 + \frac{0.07}{365}\right)^{91} = \$1017.60$$

However, over one full year this difference disappears when rounding to the nearest cent, as is shown by the next two equations.

$$A = (\$1000.00)\left(1 + \frac{0.07}{366}\right)^{366} = \$1072.50$$

$$A = (\$1000.00)\left(1 + \frac{0.07}{365}\right)^{365} = \$1072.50$$

There is one more common method of compounding interest. It is called **continuous compounding**. This type of compounding is roughly comparable to compounding interest every second of the day with no round off. That is, for a principal P, at an annual percentage rate R and time T, the balance is

$$A = P(e^{RT}).$$

The number e is approximately equal to 2.71828. Therefore, we can say that

$$A = P(e^{RT}) \approx P(2.71828)^{RT}.$$

[The formula $A \approx P(2.71828)^{RT}$ is convenient to use if your calculator does not happen to have the $[e^x]$ function. It serves as a close approximation to $A = P(e^{RT})$.]

Calculator Hints

$A = P(e^{RT})$

To find the amount of continuously compounded interest using your calculator, apply the following steps:

1. Multiply R by t and press $\boxed{=}$.

2. Press $\boxed{\text{2nd}}$ then $\boxed{\div}$.*

3. Multiply by P.

4. Round to the nearest cent.

* On the Explorer Plus™ Calculator, pressing $\boxed{\text{2nd}}$ then $\boxed{\div}$ is equivlent to pressing $[e^x]$ on some other calculator models.

EXAMPLE 4 **Finding interest by continuous compounding**

Suppose that Ray Patton's deposit (see previous Examples) of $1000.00 at $3\frac{1}{4}\%$ is compounded continuously.

a. What is Ray's balance at the end of one year?

b. What is Ray's balance at the end of four years?

SOLUTION

a. Since $P = \$1000.00$ and $R = 0.0325$, we have a balance at the end of one year of

$$A = P(e^{RT}) = (\$1000.00)[e^{(0.0325)(1)}] \approx \$1033.03,$$

which is the same balance Ray had in Example 3 with daily compounding.

b. At the end of four years, we would have $T = 4$ and the balance would be

$$A = P(e^{RT}) = (\$1000.00)[e^{(0.0325)(4)}] \approx \$1138.83.$$

EXAMPLE 4b

Steps	Display
0.0325 ☒ 4 ☐	0.13
2nd ÷	1.138828383
☒ 1000 ☐	1138.828383

Thus, with continuous compounding, Ray received one cent more interest over a period of four years than was earned with daily compounding. ◆

Try one!

Andrew Winstead deposited $1500.00 in a four-year certificate of deposit at $4\frac{1}{4}\%$ compounded continuously. Find Andrew's balance **a)** at the end of one year, and **b)** at the end of four years.

One Year: _____

Four Years: _____

By comparing Examples 1–4, we can see that the differences between daily and continuous compounding are very slight. For small deposits over short periods of time, the two compounding methods usually yield identical balances. Table 5 compares the balances obtained by depositing $1000.00 at various rates, compoundings, and periods of time. Notice that the longer the time period, the more you benefit from a higher rate or more frequent compoundings.

TABLE 5   BALANCE FOR $1000.00 AT VARIOUS INTEREST RATES, COMPOUNDINGS, AND TIMES

Annual Percentage Rate	Type of Compounding	Number of Years					
		1	2	4	6	8	10
3%	Annual	$1030.00	$1060.90	$1125.51	$1194.05	$1266.77	$1343.92
	Quarterly	$1030.34	$1061.60	$1126.99	$1196.41	$1270.11	$1348.35
	Monthly	$1030.42	$1061.76	$1127.33	$1196.95	$1270.87	$1349.35
	Daily	$1030.45	$1061.83	$1127.49	$1197.21	$1271.24	$1349.84
	Continuously	$1030.45	$1061.84	$1127.50	$1197.22	$1271.25	$1349.86
4%	Annual	$1040.00	$1081.60	$1169.86	$1265.32	$1368.57	$1480.24
	Quarterly	$1040.60	$1082.86	$1172.58	$1269.73	$1374.94	$1488.86
	Monthly	$1040.74	$1083.14	$1173.20	$1270.74	$1376.39	$1490.83
	Daily	$1040.81	$1083.28	$1173.50	$1271.23	$1377.10	$1491.79
	Continuously	$1040.81	$1083.29	$1173.51	$1271.25	$1377.13	$1491.82
5%	Annual	$1050.00	$1102.50	$1215.51	$1340.10	$1477.46	$1628.89
	Quarterly	$1050.95	$1104.49	$1219.89	$1347.35	$1488.13	$1643.62
	Monthly	$1051.16	$1104.94	$1220.90	$1349.02	$1490.59	$1647.01
	Daily	$1051.27	$1105.16	$1221.39	$1349.83	$1491.78	$1648.66
	Continuously	$1051.27	$1105.17	$1221.40	$1349.86	$1491.82	$1648.72
6%	Annual	$1060.00	$1123.60	$1262.48	$1418.52	$1593.85	$1790.85
	Quarterly	$1061.36	$1126.49	$1268.99	$1429.50	$1610.32	$1814.02
	Monthly	$1061.68	$1127.16	$1270.49	$1432.04	$1614.14	$1819.40
	Daily	$1061.83	$1127.49	$1271.22	$1433.29	$1616.01	$1822.03
	Continuously	$1061.84	$1127.50	$1271.25	$1433.33	$1616.07	1822.12$
7%	Annual	$1070.00	$1144.90	$1310.80	$1500.73	$1718.19	$1967.15
	Quarterly	$1071.86	$1148.88	$1319.93	$1516.44	$1742.21	$2001.60
	Monthly	$1072.29	$1149.81	$1322.05	$1520.11	$1747.83	$2009.66
	Daily	$1072.50	$1150.26	$1323.09	$1521.90	$1750.58	$2013.62
	Continuously	$1072.51	$1150.27	$1323.13	$1521.96	$1750.67	$2013.75
8%	Annual	$1080.00	$1166.40	$1360.49	$1586.87	$1850.93	$2158.92
	Quarterly	$1082.43	$1171.66	$1372.79	$1608.44	$1884.54	$2208.04
	Monthly	$1083.00	$1172.89	$1375.67	$1613.50	$1892.46	$2219.64
	Daily	$1083.28	$1173.49	$1377.08	$1615.99	$1896.35	$2225.35
	Continuously	$1083.29	$1173.51	$1377.13	$1616.07	$1896.48	$2225.54

Most passbook savings accounts compound interest daily from the day-of-deposit to the day-of-withdrawal. After each deposit or withdrawal, the balance in the account changes according to the following formula:

$$\begin{matrix} \text{Balance After} \\ \text{Deposit} \\ \text{or Withdrawal} \end{matrix} = \begin{matrix} \text{Balance After} \\ \text{Previous Deposit} \\ \text{or Withdrawal} \end{matrix} + \text{Deposits} - \text{Withdrawals} + \begin{matrix} \text{Interest on} \\ \text{Previous Balance} \end{matrix}$$

The interest over any period of time is given by

$$\text{Interest} = \text{Ending Balance} - \text{Beginning Balance} - \text{Deposits} + \text{Withdrawals}$$

| | EXAMPLE 5 | | **Finding the balance and interest for a passbook savings account** |

EXAMPLE 5 — Finding the balance and interest for a passbook savings account

Fran Trevor has a passbook savings account that pays $5\frac{1}{2}\%$ compounded daily. Her balance on January 1 was $1048.60. During the year, she deposited $250.00 on March 4, $300.00 on July 12, and withdrew $400.00 on December 1. (Assume the year is not a leap year.)

a. What is Fran's balance on January 1 of the following year?

b. How much interest did Fran earn during the year?

SOLUTION

a. To determine Fran's balance, we break the year into four periods according to Fran's deposits and withdrawals as shown below.

Date	Deposit	Withdrawal	Number of Days
January 1	–	–	62
March 4	$250.00	–	130
July 12	$300.00	–	142
December 1	–	$400.00	31
			Total = 365 days

Now, from *January 1 to March 4*, Fran would earn 62 days' interest on a beginning balance of $1048.60, which would give her a balance of

$$A = P\left(1 + \frac{R}{365}\right)^N = (\$1048.60)\left(1 + \frac{0.055}{365}\right)^{62} \approx \$1058.44.$$

Since Fran deposited $250.00 on March 4, her balance then would be

$$A = \$1058.44 + \$250.00 = \$1308.44.$$

From *March 4 to July 12*, Fran's balance would grow to

$$A = P\left(1 + \frac{R}{365}\right)^N = (\$1308.44)\left(1 + \frac{0.055}{365}\right)^{130} \approx \$1334.32$$

and her additional deposit of $300.00 would leave her with a July 12 balance of

$$A = \$1334.32 + \$300.00 = \$1634.32.$$

From *July 12 to December 1*, Fran's balance would grow to

$$A = P\left(1 + \frac{R}{365}\right)^N = (\$1634.32)\left(1 + \frac{0.055}{365}\right)^{142} \approx \$1669.66$$

and her $400.00 withdrawal would leave Fran with a December 1 balance of

$$A = \$1669.66 - \$400.00 = \$1269.66.$$

Finally, from *December 1 to January 1*, Fran's balance would grow to

$$A = P\left(1 + \frac{R}{365}\right)^N = (\$1269.66)\left(1 + \frac{0.055}{365}\right)^{31} \approx \$1275.60.$$

b. To find Fran's total interest earned during the year, we use the formula

$$\text{Interest} = \begin{matrix} \text{Ending} \\ \text{Balance} \end{matrix} - \begin{matrix} \text{Beginning} \\ \text{Balance} \end{matrix} - \text{Deposits} + \text{Withdrawals}$$

$$= \$1275.60 - \$1048.60 - \$550.00 + \$400.00$$

$$= \$77.00.$$

The year's record of posting in Fran's account is shown below.

Date	Deposit	Withdrawal	Interest	Balance
Jan. 1	–	–	–	$1048.60
Mar. 4	$250.00	–	$9.84	$1308.44
July 12	$300.00	–	$25.88	$1634.32
Dec. 1	–	$400.00	$35.34	$1269.66
Jan.1	–	–	$5.94	$1275.60
			Total = $77.00	

◆

Try one!

Jason King has a passbook savings account that pays 4% compounded daily. His balance on January 1 was $1075.50. During the year, he deposited $350.00 on April 4, and withdrew $300.00 on December 15. (Assume the year is not a leap year.)

a. What is Jason's balance on January 1 of the following year?

Answer: _____

b. How much interest did Jason earn during the year?

Answer: _____

The advantage of a day-of-deposit to day-of-withdrawal account is its flexibility. You may add or take away any amount and still earn interest for every day you leave the money in the account. The disadvantage of this type of savings account is that the interest rate is usually lower than the rates for savings accounts that have less flexibility.

If you put your money in an account that pays interest on a basis other than day-of-deposit to day-of-withdrawal, be sure you understand the penalty policies. By not conforming precisely to the stated policies, you can drastically reduce your annual effective yield. For instance, to some savings institutions, quarterly compounding means compounding *only* on January 1, March 1, July 1, and September 1 with no interest earned on balances held on deposit for less than a full calendar quarter. In such an account, money deposited on January 15 and withdrawn the following December 15 would draw interest only during the second and third quarters even though it was on deposit for eleven months. By depositing on January 15 instead of January 1, the depositor suffered a *penalty for late deposit* and by withdrawing on December 15 instead of January 1, the account holder suffered a *penalty for early withdrawal*. Of these two types of penalties, the penalty for early withdrawal is the most common and often the most severe. Although penalties for early withdrawal differ from one institution to another, a typical penalty is described in Example 6.

EXAMPLE 6 Finding the penalty for early withdrawal

Carla and Tim Grant purchased a 6-year savings certificate for $2000.00, compounded quarterly at $4\frac{1}{2}\%$. The penalty for early withdrawal is the loss of interest for the two most recent quarters.

a. What penalty would Carla and Tim be given if they withdrew their money after six months?

b. What penalty would Carla and Tim be given if they withdrew their money after one year? What is their annual effective yield in this case?

SOLUTION

If left to full maturity, Carla and Tim's $2000.00 would have earned the following interest during the first year.

Quarter	Principal	Interest	Balance
1	$2000.00	$22.50	$2022.50
2	$2022.50	$22.75	$2045.25
3	$2045.25	$23.01	$2068.26
4	$2068.26	$23.25	$2091.51

a. If Carla and Tim withdraw the $2000.00 after six months, they will lose the interest for the first two quarters. In other words, they would receive no interest and their penalty would be

$$\text{Penalty} = \text{loss of first two quarters' interest} = \$22.50 + \$22.75 = \$45.25.$$

b. If Carla and Tim withdraw the $2000.00 after one year, they will lost the third and fourth quarters' interest. Their penalty would be

$$\text{Penalty} = \text{loss of third and fourth quarters' interest} = \$23.01 + \$23.25 = \$46.26.$$

Their interest would be

$$I = \$22.50 + \$22.75 = \$45.25$$

which means that their annual effective yield is

$$Y = \frac{I}{P} = \frac{\$45.25}{\$2000.00} \approx 0.0226 = 2.26\%. \qquad \blacklozenge$$

Try one!

Bill and Samantha Dobson purchased a two-year savings certificate for $3000.00 compounded quarterly at $3\frac{3}{4}\%$. The penalty for early withdrawal is the loss of interest for the two most recent quarters.

a. What penalty would Carla and Tim be given if they withdrew their money after nine months?

Answer: _____

b. What penalty would Carla and Tim be given if they withdrew their money after one year? What is their annual effective yield in this case?

Answer: _____

Effective Yield: _____

Most commercial banks have one or more types of checking accounts for which the customer pays no service charge. For example, a bank may be willing to offer "no charge checking" to everyone who keeps a minimum balance of $500.00 in a passbook savings account, or an average monthly balance of $200.00 in a regular checking account, or any number of other requirements. In addition to "no charge checking," banks offer interest on the daily balance in checking accounts. These interest-earning checking accounts are called **NOW** accounts (*negotiable order of withdrawal*) or **automatic savings transfer** accounts. In order to benefit from an interest-earning checking account, the account holder must keep a fairly large minimum balance in the account. If the minimum is not maintained, the monthly service charge can be quite high.

Some people like to maintain a balance of several hundred dollars in either their passbook savings or their regular checking account so that they won't be caught off their guard in case of an emergency. For such people, interest-earning checking accounts are a good idea since the money earns interest that they would not have otherwise received. Other account holders figure that the unexpected occasions for which they need large sums of money are so rare that they would rather keep their money in long-term savings accounts that pay higher interest rates, even though in this case the money is not readily accessible without substantial penalty. Example 7 describes such a case.

EXAMPLE 7   Comparing a regular checking account to an interest earning account

Rick Norris deposits $1500.00 per month in his regular checking account for which he pays no service charge since his average balance in the account is $500.00. If Rick changed to an interest-earning checking account, he could earn $3\frac{1}{4}\%$ daily interest on his checking balance just as if it were in a passbook account. Rick figures that this interest would amount to approximately $1.38 per month. However, in order to qualify for the new checking account (it requires $1000.00 minimum balance in order to be service-charge free) Rick would have to sell a $1000.00 bond that pays 6% simple interest each year. Which plan would give Rick more interest at the end of the year?

SOLUTION

If Rick keeps the $1000.00 bond and earns no interest on his checking account, his bond would pay interest amounting to

$$I = PRT = (\$1000.00)(0.06)(1) = \$60.00.$$

If Rick puts the $1000.00 into a new interest-earning checking account, it would earn $3\frac{1}{4}\%$ compounded daily which at the end of a year would amount to

$$A = P\left(1 + \frac{R}{365}\right)^N = (\$1000)\left(1 + \frac{0.0325}{365}\right)^{365} = \$1033.03.$$

In addition to the $3\frac{1}{4}\%$ interest Rick earns on the $1000.00, he would earn approximately $1.38 per month on that portion of his paycheck that remained in the account during the month. At the end of the year, this would amount to

$$\text{Interest} = (12)(\$1.38) = \$16.56$$

resulting in a total yearly interest of

$$I = \$33.03 + \$16.56 = \$49.59.$$

Therefore, in Rick's particular situation, it is slightly better to keep a smaller balance in his regular checking account than to keep a larger balance in an interest-earning checking account. ◆

Important Terms

compound interest A, amount or balance

continuous compounding   nominal rate

automatic savings transfer   NOW account

T. time P, principal

Y, annual effective yield

n, number of compoundings per year

N, total number of compoundings

penalty for early withdrawal

Important Formulas

Annual Compounding   Quarterly Compounding

$$A = P(1 + R)^N$$ $$A = P\left(1 + \frac{R}{4}\right)^N$$

Monthly Compounding   Daily Compounding

$$A = P\left(1 + \frac{R}{12}\right)^N$$ $$A = P\left(1 + \frac{R}{365}\right)^N$$

Continuous Compounding

$$A = P(e^{RT}) \approx P(2.71828)^{RT}$$

CONSUMER HINTS

• Interest rates are strictly regulated by the federal government. When shopping for the best rate on a savings account, be sure to consider different types of savings institutions (credit unions, savings and loan associations, commercial banks, etc.).

• For savings accounts other than day-of-deposit to day-of-withdrawal, be sure that you understand the penalty system for early withdrawal. If you are not sure that you can wait for a long-term savings certificate to reach full maturity, it might be better to accept a lower rate for a short time.

• Remember that the longer the term of deposit, the more you have to gain from higher rates and more frequent compoundings.

• If you normally keep a large balance in a regular savings account or a regular checking account, it may be to your advantage to change your checking account to one that earns interest.

SECTION 2 EXERCISES

In Exercises 1-4, **a.** complete the quarterly balance record for a year, and **b.** find the annual effective yield.

1. $500.00 deposited in a savings account paying 3% compounded quarterly.

a.

Quarter	Principal	Interest	Balance
1	$500.00	_____	_____
2	_____	_____	_____
3	_____	_____	_____
4	_____	_____	_____

b.   Annual effective yield: _____

2. $2000.00 deposited in a savings account paying 5% compounded quarterly.

a.

Quarter	Principal	Interest	Balance
1	$2000.00	_____	_____
2	_____	_____	_____
3	_____	_____	_____
4	_____	_____	_____

b.   Annual effective yield: _____

3. $5000.00 deposited in a savings account paying 6% compounded quarterly.

a.	Quarter	Principal	Interest	Balance
	1	$5000.00	_____	_____
	2	_____	_____	_____
	3	_____	_____	_____
	4	_____	_____	_____

b.   Annual effective yield: _____

4. $3375.00 deposited in a savings account paying $4\frac{1}{2}\%$ compounded quarterly.

a.

Quarter	Principal	Interest	Balance
1	$3375.00	_____	_____
2	_____	_____	_____
3	_____	_____	_____
4	_____	_____	_____

b.   Annual effective yield: _____

5. Complete the following table for a deposit of $500.00 at 3% for one year.

Number of Compoundings Per Year	1	4	12	365	Continuously
Balance After One Year	_____	_____	_____	_____	_____
Annual Effective Yield	_____	_____	_____	_____	_____

6. Complete the following table for a deposit of $2000.00 at 5% for one year.

Number of Compoundings Per Year	1	4	12	365	Continuously
Balance After One Year	_____	_____	_____	_____	_____
Annual Effective Yield	_____	_____	_____	_____	_____

7. Complete the following table for a deposit of $5000.00 at 6% for one year.

Number of Compoundings Per Year	1	4	12	365	Continuously
Balance After One Year	_____	_____	_____	_____	_____
Annual Effective Yield	_____	_____	_____	_____	_____

8. Complete the following table for a deposit of $3375.00 at $4\frac{1}{2}\%$ for one year.

Number of Compoundings Per Year	1	4	12	365	Continuously
Balance After One Year	_____	_____	_____	_____	_____
Annual Effective Yield	_____	_____	_____	_____	_____

9. Complete the following table for a deposit of $300.00 at $5\frac{1}{2}$% for two years.

Number of Compoundings Per Year	1	4	12	365	Continuously
Balance After Two Years	_____	_____	_____	_____	_____

10. Complete the following table for a deposit of $750.00 at 6% for five years.

Number of Compoundings Per Year	1	4	12	365	Continuously
Balance After Five Years	_____	_____	_____	_____	_____

10,000 $4\frac{1}{2}$%   10

11. Complete the following table for a deposit of ~~$300.00~~ at ~~$5\frac{1}{2}$~~% for ~~two~~ years.

Number of Compoundings Per Year	1	4	12	365	Continuously
Balance After Two Years	_____	_____	_____	_____	_____

12. Complete the following table for a deposit of $10,000.00 at $4\frac{1}{2}\%$ for 20 years.

Number of Compoundings Per Year	1	4	12	365	Continuously
Balance After 20 Years	_____	_____	_____	_____	_____

13. Complete the following table for a deposit of $10,000.00 at $4\frac{1}{2}\%$ for 25 years.

Number of Compoundings Per Year	1	4	12	365	Continuously
Balance After 25 Years	_____	_____	_____	_____	_____

14. Complete the following table for a deposit of $500.00 at 7% for 50 years.

Number of Compoundings Per Year	1	4	12	365	Continuously
Balance After 50 Years	_____	_____	_____	_____	_____

In Exercises 15–18, use Table 5 to find the amount for each savings plan.

15. $2000.00 at 6% compounded monthly for eight years.

Answer: _____

16. $5000.00 at 4% compounded daily for four years.

Answer: _____

17. $500.00 at 5% compounded continuously for four years.

Answer: _____

18. $250.00 at 7% compounded quarterly for six years.

Answer: _____

19. Dorothy Newmeyer has a passbook savings account that pays 6% compounded daily. Her balance on January 1 is $3162.47. During that year, she deposited $422.50 on February 16, $150.00 on August 28, and withdrew $1250.00 on July 14. (Assume a non leap year.)

  a. What is Dorothy's balance on January 1 of the following year?

  Answer: _____

  b. How much interest did Dorothy's account earn during the year?

  Answer: _____

20. Bill Wilkinson has a passbook savings account that pays $6\frac{1}{2}\%$ compounded daily. His balance on January 1 was \$1630.47. During the year he deposited \$500.00 at the end of each quarter (March 31, June 30, September 30, December 31) and withdrew \$250.00 on April 8 and \$632.00 on August 10. (Assume a non leap year.)

a. What is Bill's balance on January 1 of the following year?

Answer: _____

b. How much interest did Bill's account earn during the year?

Answer: _____

21. Marcia Nelson has a four-year savings certificate for $1000.00 compounded monthly at 5%. The penalty for early withdrawal is the loss of interest for the three most recent months. What penalty would Marcia be given if she withdraws the money at the end of the third year?

Answer: _____

22. John Buckley has a six-year savings certificate for $5000.00 compounded daily at $4\frac{1}{2}\%$. The penalty for early withdrawal is the loss of interest for the most recent 180 days. What penalty would John be given if he withdrew his money after four years?

Answer: _____

23. Joyce Oakley wants to set aside an amount now so that there will be $5000.00 available for her daughter to start college in ten years. What amount should she invest now at $\frac{3}{4}$% compounded daily? (Hint: Solve for P in the given formula.)

$$A = P\left(1 + \frac{R}{365}\right)^N$$

Answer: _____

24. What principal invested now at $5\frac{1}{2}$% compounded continuously will yield an amount of $10,000.00 in the following number of years. [Hint: Solve for P in the formula $A = P(e^{RT})$.]

  a. Four years

Answer: _____

  b. Five years

Answer: _____

  c. Ten years

Answer: _____

25. If a certain principal P is invested now at 9% compounded monthly, the amount after N compoundings is $A = P\left(1 + \dfrac{0.09}{12}\right)^N = P(1.0075)^N$. By trial and error, using the $\boxed{y^x}$ key, approximate the time necessary to **a.** double the original investment, and **b.** triple the original investment.

Double: _____

Triple: _____

Section 3
Increasing Annuities

In Sections 1 and 2, we looked at two methods of saving money: single-deposit, long-term accounts such as savings certificates and bonds, and day-of-deposit to day-of-withdrawal accounts such as passbook accounts or interest-earning checking accounts. A third basic method of saving is called an **increasing annuity**. An annuity is characterized by many equal deposits (or withdrawals) at regular intervals over a long period of time. A typical example of an annuity is a payroll savings plan in which a fixed amount of an employee's paycheck is deducted each pay period and placed in savings. Example 1 describes such a situation.

EXAMPLE 1   Constructing an annuity table

Wanda Kruger works for a large manufacturer and is a member of the employee credit union. Each month, through a payroll savings plan, Wanda deposits $25.00 in her credit union savings account. If Wanda's account pays $6\frac{1}{2}\%$ compounded monthly, how much would Wanda have in her account at the end of the first year? How much interest would she have earned in the year?

SOLUTION

After having $25.00 on deposit for one month, Wanda would have earned interest of

$$I = PRT = (\$25.00)(0.065)(\tfrac{1}{12}) \approx \$0.14$$

leaving a balance of $25.14. Now, at the beginning of the second month, Wanda's second deposit would bring her principal up to $50.14 which by the end of the second month would earn an interest of

$$I = PRT = (\$50.14)(0.065)(\tfrac{1}{12}) \approx \$0.27$$

leaving a balance of $50.41. Continuing this procedure, we have the record of Wanda's account shown in Table 6.

TABLE 6	ANNUITY TABLE FOR $25.00 PER MONTH FOR ONE YEAR AT $6\frac{1}{2}\%$			
Deposit Number	Deposit	Principal	Interest	Balance
1	$25.00	$25.00	$0.14	$25.14
2	$25.00	$50.14	$0.27	$50.41
3	$25.00	$75.41	$0.41	$75.82
4	$25.00	$100.82	$0.55	$101.37
5	$25.00	$126.37	$0.68	$127.05
6	$25.00	$152.05	$0.82	$152.87
7	$25.00	$177.87	$0.96	$178.83
8	$25.00	$203.83	$1.10	$204.93
9	$25.00	$229.93	$1.25	$231.18
10	$25.00	$256.18	$1.39	$257.57
11	$25.00	$282.57	$1.53	$284.10
12	$25.00	$309.10	$1.67	$310.77

From Table 6, we see that Wanda's balance at the end of the year is $310.77 and the interest earned during the year totals $10.77. ◆

Try one!

Bryan Wills deposits $100.00 in his savings account at the end of each quarter. If Bryan's account pays $3\frac{1}{2}\%$ compounded quarterly, construct an annuity table to determine how much Bryan would have in his account at the end of the first year. How much interest would he have earned in the year?

Deposit Number	Deposit	Principal	Interest	Balance
1	$100.00	$_____	$_____	$_____
2	$_____	$_____	$_____	$_____
3	$_____	$_____	$_____	$_____
4	$_____	$_____	$_____	$_____

Total Interest: _____

Calculator Hints

$$A = P\left[\left(1 + \frac{R}{n}\right)^N - 1\right]\left(1 + \frac{n}{R}\right)$$

To find the balance of an increasing annuity using your calculator, apply the following steps:

1. Divide n by R, add 1 and store the result.
2. Divide R by n and add 1.
3. Raise to the Nth power and subtract 1.
4. Multiply by the value stored in step 1.
5. Multiply by P.
6. Round to nearest cent.

The formula for finding the balance of an increasing annuity after a total of N deposits with n deposits per year is

$$A = P\left[\left(1 + \frac{R}{n}\right)^N - 1\right]\left(1 + \frac{n}{R}\right)$$

where

P = periodic deposit

R = annual percentage rate (compounded n times per year)

N = *total* number of deposits

n = number of deposits *per year*

A = balance after N deposits.

EXAMPLE 2   **Finding the balance of a monthly annuity by formula**

In Example 1, Wanda Kruger deposited $25.00 per month at $6\frac{1}{2}\%$ compounded monthly. Use the formula for the balance of an increasing annuity to find the balance in Wanda's account

a. at the end of one year

b. at the end of two years

c. at the end of five years.

SOLUTION

a. Since $P = \$25.00$, $R = 0.065$, $n = 12$, and $N = 12$, Wanda's balance at the end of one year is

$$A = P\left[\left(1 + \frac{R}{n}\right)^N - 1\right]\left(1 + \frac{n}{R}\right)$$

$$= (\$25.00)\left[\left(1 + \frac{0.065}{12}\right)^{12} - 1\right]\left(1 + \frac{12}{0.065}\right).$$

Therefore, the balance at the end of one year is $310.78. (Note that as in Section 2, the table method in Example 1 may produce balances which differ slightly from the balances obtained by formula.)

EXAMPLE 2a

Steps	Display
12 ÷ 0.065 =	184.6153846
+ 1 = STO	185.6153846
0.065 ÷ 12 =	0.005416667
+ 1 =	1.005416667
yˣ 12 =	1.066971852
− 1 =	0.066971852
× RCL =	12.43100608
× 25 =	310.7751519

b. At the end of two years, $N = 24$, and the balance is

$$A = P\left[\left(1 + \frac{R}{n}\right)^N - 1\right]\left(1 + \frac{n}{R}\right)$$

$$= (\$25.00)\left[\left(1 + \frac{0.065}{12}\right)^{24} - 1\right]\left(1 + \frac{12}{0.065}\right)$$

$$\approx \$642.36.$$

c. At the end of five years, $N = 5(12) = 60$, and the balance is

$$A = P\left[\left(1 + \frac{R}{N}\right)^N - 1\right]\left(1 + \frac{n}{R}\right)$$

$$= (\$25.00)\left[\left(1 + \frac{0.065}{12}\right)^{60} - 1\right]\left(1 + \frac{12}{0.065}\right)$$

$$\approx \$1776.42. \qquad\qquad\qquad\qquad\blacklozenge$$

Try one!

Bryan Wills deposited $100.00 per month at $3\frac{1}{2}\%$ compounded monthly. Use the formula for the balance of an increasing annuity to find the balance in Bryan's account for the following:

a. At the end of one year

Answer: _____

b. At the end of two years

Answer: _____

Keep in mind that n is the number of deposits *per year* and N is the *total* number of deposits. The increasing annuity formulas for the most common values of n are

$$\text{Annual: } A = P\left[(1 + R)^N - 1\right]\left(1 + \frac{1}{R}\right)$$

$$\text{Quarterly: } A = P\left[\left(1 + \frac{R}{4}\right)^N - 1\right]\left(1 + \frac{4}{R}\right)$$

$$\text{Monthly: } A = P\left[\left(1 + \frac{R}{12}\right)^N - 1\right]\left(1 + \frac{12}{R}\right)$$

$$\text{Biweekly: } A = P\left[\left(1 + \frac{R}{26}\right)^N - 1\right]\left(1 + \frac{26}{R}\right)$$

$$\text{Weekly: } A = P\left[\left(1 + \frac{R}{52}\right)^N - 1\right]\left(1 + \frac{52}{R}\right).$$

In each case, we assume the interest is compounded at the time of deposit.

| EXAMPLE 3 | **Finding the balance of an increasing annuity by formula** |

Linda and Curt Anderson purchased a $1000.00 savings certificate every year for 17 years. If the interest rate for their increasing annuity was 5.478%, compounded annually, what was their balance at the end of 17 years?

SOLUTION

For an annual annuity, with $P = \$1000.00$, $R = 0.05478$, $n = 1$, and $N = 17$, the balance is

$$A = P\left[(1 + R)^N - 1\right]\left(1 + \frac{1}{R}\right)$$

$$= (\$1000.00)\left[(1 + 0.05478)^{17} - 1\right]\left(1 + \frac{1}{0.05478}\right)$$

$$\approx \$28,420.30. \qquad \blacklozenge$$

Try one!

John and Wendy Monroe decide to purchase a $2500.00 savings certificate every year for 12 years. The interest rate for this certificate is $3\frac{3}{4}\%$, compounded annually. What will their balance be at the end of 12 years?

Answer: _____

Since many people are paid every other week, the biweekly annuity is one of the most common. Table 7 shows the rate of growth for a *biweekly increasing annuity* for different rates, terms, and deposits.

TABLE 7 — BALANCE OF ANNUITIES FOR VARIOUS RATES, BIWEEKLY DEPOSITS, AND TERMS

Annual Percentage Rate	Biweekly Deposit	Number of Years				
		1	5	10	15	20
5%	$10.00	$266.86	$1478.17	$3375.71	$5811.63	$8938.65
	$25.00	$667.15	$3695.42	$8439.29	$14,529.07	$22,346.64
	$50.00	$1334.30	$7390.83	$16,878.57	$29,058.15	$44,693.27
	$100.00	$2668.59	$14,781.67	$33,757.14	$58,116.29	$89,386.55
$5\frac{1}{2}\%$	$10.00	$267.56	$1497.68	$3468.85	$6063.20	$9477.76
	$25.00	$668.89	$3744.20	$8672.13	$15,158.01	$23,694.39
	$50.00	$1337.79	$7488.40	$17,344.26	$30,316.02	$47,388.78
	$100.00	$2675.58	$14,976.81	$34,688.51	$60,632.04	$94,777.56
6%	$10.00	$268.26	$1517.53	$3565.27	$6328.47	$10,057.12
	$25.00	$670.64	$3793.82	$8913.17	$15,821.18	$25,142.80
	$50.00	$1341.29	$7587.64	$17,826.34	$31,642.36	$50,285.59
	$100.00	$2682.58	$15,175.27	$35,652.67	$63,284.72	$100,571.19
$6\frac{1}{2}\%$	$10.00	$268.96	$1537.71	$3665.09	$6608.25	$10,680.03
	$25.00	$672.40	$3844.28	$9162.73	$16,520.63	$26,700.07
	$50.00	$1344.80	$7688.56	$18,325.45	$33,041.27	$53,400.14
	$100.00	$2689.61	$15,377.12	$36,650.91	$66,082.53	$106,800.29
7%	$10.00	$269.67	$1558.24	$3768.45	$6903.42	$11,350.05
	$25.00	$674.16	$3895.61	$9421.13	$17,258.54	$28,375.13
	$50.00	$1348.33	$7791.21	$18,842.27	$34,517.09	$56,750.26
	$100.00	$2696.65	$15,582.42	$37,684.54	$69,034.18	$113,500.52

EXAMPLE 4   **Finding the balance of an increasing annuity**

Judith and Christopher Rinehart graduated in 1980 at age 25 with advanced degrees and both accepted jobs with high salaries. In 1981, they each paid the maximum social security contribution of $3950.10 split between themselves and their employers. Instead of paying into the social security plan, suppose that Judith and Christopher were allowed to deposit this amount each year in a savings account at 7% for 40 years, compounded annually. How much would they have in the account at age 65?

SOLUTION

The combined social security contribution paid by Judith, Christopher and their employers on their behalf is

   Annual contribution = 2($3950.10) = $7900.20.

Using $P = \$7900.20$, $R = 0.07$, $n = 1$, and $N = 40$, we have a balance at the end of 40 years of

$$A = P\left[(1 + R)^N - 1\right]\left(1 + \frac{1}{R}\right)$$

$$= (\$7900.20)\left[(1 + 0.07)^{40} - 1\right]\left(1 + \frac{1}{0.07}\right)$$

$$\approx \$1,687,558.32.$$

For a balance of this magnitude, the interest alone (at 7% per year) could give Judith and Christopher a retirement income of $118,129.08 per year for life without dipping into their balance of nearly 1.7 million dollars. (If the interest rate during the 40 years had been 9% instead of 7%, the final balance would be $2,909,579.39.)   ◆

Example 4 dramatically illustrates the potential as well as the failure of the present social security system in the United States. Although many people making social security contributions believe that they are paying into an increasing annuity type of retirement plan, this is not the case. In practice, social security contributions are not set aside to gain interest for the contributor's retirement, but are paid out each year to current recipients of the system.

Try one!

Suppose that at age 35 Judith and Christopher decided to deposit $2000.00 each year in a savings account at $4\frac{3}{4}\%$ for 30 years, compounded annually. How much would they have in the account at age 65?

Answer: _____

A common type of short-term increasing annuity is the "target savings plan." The policies for such plans vary from one institution to another, but a popular version of the plan requires participants to make 50 weekly payments beginning in mid-November until the end of the following October. At that time, the plan participant receives a check for the amount deposited plus interest amounting to one week's deposit. If the funds are withdrawn early, or if one or more of the payments are late or missing, *no* interest is paid and the plan participant might even be assessed an additional penalty. As far as annuities go, such plans are good for banks but not as good for participants. The only practical benefit a plan participant has is that the penalty system may provide motivation for participants who have trouble saving on a regular basis. Participants who withdraw early and pay a penalty (in addition to losing their interest) would do better to put their money in a cookie jar. Better than that, they should put their money into a regular savings account as illustrated in the following example.

EXAMPLE 5   Finding the balance of a target savings plan annuity

Diane Griswald joined a target savings plan on November 6, 1992. For 50 weeks, she deposited $20.00 in her account. After the 50th week, she received one week's "free" deposit as her interest for the year. If she had put the same amount in a day-of-deposit to day-of-withdrawal account paying $4\frac{1}{4}\%$ compounded weekly, how much would she have at the end of the 50 weeks?

SOLUTION

For the target savings plan, Diane would receive $1020.00 after 50 weeks. In a savings account paying $4\frac{1}{4}\%$, using $P = \$20.00$, $R = 0.04$, $n = 52$, and $N = 50$, Diane would have a balance of

$$A = P\left[\left(1 + \frac{R}{52}\right)^N - 1\right]\left(1 + \frac{52}{R}\right)$$

$$= (\$20.00)\left[\left(1 + \frac{0.0425}{52}\right)^{50} - 1\right]\left(1 + \frac{52}{0.0425}\right)$$

$$\approx \$1021.12.$$

Therefore, Diane would do better by putting her money in a regular savings account at $4\frac{1}{4}\%$. Not only would she earn more interest, but she could also withdraw early or miss payments and still draw interest on a day-of-deposit to day-of-withdrawal basis. Keep in mind, however, that the interest rate on the regular savings account influences the outcome of this example. For instance, at 4% interest, Diane would only earn $1019.86 in her regular savings account and at $3\frac{3}{4}\%$ she would earn only $1018.61. In both of these cases, the target savings plan yields a larger end balance than does the regular savings account. It is therefore very important to consider the current interest rates at your bank as well as the type of savings plan that would be most beneficial to your particular situation. ◆

Try one!

Barb Stewart is trying to decide whether or not to open a target savings plan account. She would have to make 50 weekly deposits of $25.00 in order to receive one week's "free" deposit as her interest for the year. If her bank's regular savings account is a day-of-deposit to day-of-withdrawal account at $4\frac{1}{2}\%$ interest compounded weekly, determine which savings plan would have the greater yield at the end of the 50 weeks.

Answer: _____

Calculator Hints

$$P = \frac{A}{\left[\left(1 + \frac{R}{n}\right)^N - 1\right]\left(1 + \frac{n}{R}\right)}$$

To find the periodic deposit required to produce a given balance using your calculator, apply the following steps:

1. Divide n by R, add 1, and store the result.
2. Divide R by n and add 1.
3. Raise to Nth power and subtract 1.
4. Multiply by the value stored in step 1.
5. Press $\boxed{1/x}$.
6. Multiply by A.
7. Round to the nearest cent.

Many times, people want to save a specific amount over a known period of time and need to know how much they should set aside each week or month in an annuity type of savings account in order to meet their goal. To determine this, we can use the increasing annuity balance formula and solve for the periodic deposit P in terms of A, R, n, and N.

$$P = \frac{A}{\left[\left(1 + \frac{R}{n}\right)^N - 1\right]\left(1 + \frac{n}{R}\right)}$$

EXAMPLE 6 **Finding the periodic deposit required to produce a given balance**

Jim and Sherrie Zimmerly want to save $10,000.00 for a down payment on their first house.

a. How much should they set aside each month in a savings account paying $5\frac{1}{2}\%$ compounded monthly in order to have a balance of $10,000.00 at the end of five years?

b. How much should they set aside in an account paying 4%?

SOLUTION

a. Using $A = \$10,000.00$, $R = 0.055$, $n = 12$, and $N = 5(12) = 60$, we have

$$P = \frac{A}{\left[\left(1 + \frac{R}{n}\right)^N - 1\right]\left(1 + \frac{n}{R}\right)}$$

$$= \frac{\$10,000.00}{\left[\left(1 + \frac{0.055}{12}\right)^{60} - 1\right]\left(1 + \frac{12}{0.055}\right)}$$

$$\approx \$144.52.$$

EXAMPLE 3

Steps	Display
12 $\div$ 0.055 $=$	218.1818182
$+$ 1 $=$ $\boxed{STO}$	219.1818182
0.055 $\div$ 12 $=$	0.004583333
$+$ 1 $=$	1.004583333
$\boxed{y^x}$ 60 $=$	1.315703772
$-$ 1 $=$	0.315703772
$\times$ $\boxed{RCL}$ $=$	69.19652681
$\boxed{1/x}$	0.014451592
$\times$ 10000 $=$	144.5159239

Thus, at $5\frac{1}{2}\%$, Jim and Sherrie should set aside $144.52 per month in order to accumulate $10,000.00 at the end of five years.

b. At 4%, Jim and Sherrie's monthly deposit should be

$$P = \frac{A}{\left[\left(1 + \frac{R}{n}\right)^N - 1\right]\left(1 + \frac{n}{R}\right)}$$

$$= \frac{\$10,000.00}{\left[\left(1 + \frac{0.04}{12}\right)^{60} - 1\right]\left(1 + \frac{12}{0.04}\right)}$$

$$\approx \$150.33. \qquad \blacklozenge$$

Try one!

Beth and Jerome Upton want to save $25,000.00 for a down payment on a new house. They plan to purchase the house in seven years.

a. How much should they set aside each month in a savings account paying $4\frac{1}{2}\%$ compounded monthly in order to have a balance of $25,000.00 at the end of seven years?

Answer: _____

b. How much should they set aside in an account paying 6%?

Answer: _____

Important Terms

A, balance after N deposits n, number of deposits per year

N, total number of deposits R, annual percentage rate

P, deposit   increasing annuity

Important Formulas

$$A = P\left[\left(1 + \frac{R}{n}\right)^{N} - 1\right]\left(1 + \frac{n}{R}\right)$$

$$P = \frac{A}{\left[\left(1 + \frac{R}{n}\right)^{N} - 1\right]\left(1 + \frac{n}{R}\right)}$$

CONSUMER HINTS

- The annual percentage rate for long-term annuities can amount to differences in final balances of several thousand dollars (see Table 7). Therefore, if you are setting up a long-term annuity, it is especially important that you shop around for the highest possible rate.

- For short-term annuities, the best rates are often available through a credit union payroll deduction plan.

- For frequent deposits (monthly, biweekly, or weekly) over a period of several years, do not leave large balances in a day-of-deposit to day-of-withdrawal type of account. As soon as your balance qualifies you for a higher interest rate, transfer your money to the higher paying account. Of course, in so doing, you must keep in mind the penalty policies of the higher paying account.

- Carefully consider all savings options available to you before selecting a target savings plan. Investigate all plan interest rates and penalties and final balances when considering savings plans.

SECTION 3 EXERCISES

1. Jack Hilbert invests $1000.00 at the beginning of each year for five years. The account earns 5% compounded annually. Complete the following annuity table for Jack's savings plan.

Deposit Number	Deposit	Principal	Interest	Balance
1	$1000.00	_____	_____	_____
2	_____	_____	_____	_____
3	_____	_____	_____	_____
4	_____	_____	_____	_____
5	_____	_____	_____	_____

2. Shirley Smith deposits $300.00 at the beginning of each quarter (January 1, April 1, July 1, and October 1) for one year. The account earns $6\frac{1}{2}\%$ compounded quarterly. Complete the following annuity table for Shirley's savings plan.

Deposit Number	Deposit	Principal	Interest	Balance
1	$300.00	_____	_____	_____
2	_____	_____	_____	_____
3	_____	_____	_____	_____
4	_____	_____	_____	_____

3. Beverly Jordon deposits $500.00 into her daughter's savings account twice a year (January 1 and July 1) for five years. The account earns 6% compounded semi-annually. Complete the following annuity table for Beverly's daughter's savings plan.

Deposit Number	Deposit	Principal	Interest	Balance
1	$500.00	_____	_____	_____
2	_____	_____	_____	_____
3	_____	_____	_____	_____
4	_____	_____	_____	_____
5	_____	_____	_____	_____
6	_____	_____	_____	_____
7	_____	_____	_____	_____
8	_____	_____	_____	_____
9	_____	_____	_____	_____
10	_____	_____	_____	_____

4. Don Sullivan deposits $100.00 at the beginning of each month for one year. The account earns $6\frac{1}{2}\%$ compounded monthly. Complete the following annuity table for Don's savings plan.

Deposit Number	Deposit	Principal	Interest	Balance
1	$100.00	_____	_____	_____
2	_____	_____	_____	_____
3	_____	_____	_____	_____
4	_____	_____	_____	_____
5	_____	_____	_____	_____
6	_____	_____	_____	_____
7	_____	_____	_____	_____
8	_____	_____	_____	_____
9	_____	_____	_____	_____
10	_____	_____	_____	_____
11	_____	_____	_____	_____
12	_____	_____	_____	_____

In Exercises 5–8, find the balance of each increasing annuity (using the balance formula).

5. A periodic, annual deposit of $2000.00 at 12% compounded annually for 15 years.

Answer: _____

6. A periodic, biweekly (every other week) deposit of $50.00 at $6\frac{1}{2}$% compounded biweekly for two years.

Answer: _____

7. A periodic, weekly deposit of $40.00 at 6% compounded weekly for five years.

Answer: _____

8. A periodic, monthly deposit of $75.00 at 4% compounded monthly for three years.

Answer: _____

9. Kim and Larry Palmer decide to deposit $40.00 a month in a savings account for their son Daniel. If the account earns 6% compounded monthly, what is the balance in Daniel's account after 15 years?

Answer: _____

10. Dave and Cindy Saunders are both working and decide to save as much as possible for the purchase of their first house in three years. If they deposit $1000.00 a month into a savings account earning $3\frac{1}{2}$% compounded monthly, how much will they have for a down payment in three years?

Answer: _____

11. Maria Keller made deposits of $200.00 at the beginning of each month for four years. The account earns 7% compounded monthly. After four years of deposits, Maria leaves the money in the account for an additional six years (without making any further deposits). Find the balance in Maria's account at the end of the ten years. (Hint: Use the annuity formula first, then apply the compound interest formula to annuity balance.)

Answer: _____

12. Joe Calkins deposited $50.00 a month for ten years into an account for his granddaughter Gretta. The account earned $3\frac{1}{2}\%$ compounded monthly. After ten years, Joe stopped making deposits and transferred the money into an eight-year savings certificate earning $5\frac{3}{4}\%$ compounded daily. How much did Gretta have in her savings account at the end of the 18 years?

Answer: _____

13. Sam Spiegel wants to accumulate $25,000.00 in five years. How much should Sam deposit each month in an increasing annuity paying $4\frac{1}{2}\%$ compounded monthly?

Answer: _____

14. Palmer Harris plans to save $15,000.00 for the purchase of a car in four years. If Palmer gets paid every other week, how much should he have deducted from each paycheck in order to build up the $15,000.00 in four years? Assume that the money earns $6\frac{1}{2}\%$ compounded biweekly.

Answer: _____

15. Sherrie Orlov wants to save $1000.00 in one year by making weekly deposits into a savings account that pays $3\frac{1}{2}\%$ compounded weekly.

    a. How much should Sherrie deposit into her account each week?

Answer: _____

    b. At the end of the year, Sherrie purchases a $1000.00 four-year savings certificate paying 5% compounded daily. How much will the certificate be worth at maturity?

Answer: _____

16. Jennifer Mullet wants to save $2000.00 for her college tuition by the end of her three-month summer vacation. How much must she deposit each week in an account paying $5\frac{1}{2}\%$ compounded weekly? Assume that Jennifer will have 14 weekly paychecks during the summer.

Answer: _____

Section 4

Decreasing Annuities

The fourth basic type of savings is called a decreasing annuity. This type of savings is characterized by an initial deposit followed by several equal withdrawals until the account is depleted. Since any money remaining in the account earns interest until it is withdrawn, the sum of the withdrawals in a decreasing annuity is always greater than the initial deposit. Example 1 illustrates a typical situation.

> **EXAMPLE 1** **Constructing a table of balances for a decreasing annuity**

Janice Hoffman's grandfather deposited $36,298.95 in a decreasing annuity for Janice's college tuition on September 1, 1991. Beginning on September 1, 1992, Janice will be sent a check for $10,000.00 each year for four years. If the account pays 4% compounded annually, construct a record of the balance in Janice's account.

SOLUTION

On September 1, 1992, the balance in Janice's account (*before* withdrawing the $10,000.00) is

$$A = P + I = P + PRT$$

$$= \$36,298.95 + (\$36,298.95)(0.04)(1)$$

$$\approx \$36,298.95 + \$1451.96$$

$$= \$37,750.91.$$

After Janice is sent the check for $10,000.00, the balance would drop to

$$A = \$37{,}750.91 - \$10{,}000.00 = \$27{,}750.91.$$

The complete record of Janice's account is shown in Table 8.

TABLE 8 **DECREASING ANNUITY TABLE**

Date	Principal	Interest	Balance Before Withdrawal	Withdrawal	Balance After Withdrawal
9/1/1991	$36,298.95	–	$36,298.95	–	$36,298.95
9/1/1992	$36,298.95	$1451.96	$37,750.91	$10,000.00	$27,750.91
9/1/1993	$27,750.91	$1110.04	$28,860.95	$10,000.00	$18,860.95
9/1/1994	$18,860.95	$754.44	$19,615.39	$10,000.00	$9615.39
9/1/1995	$9615.39	$384.62	$10,000.01	$10,000.01	$0.00

◆

Try one!

Fred Decker deposited $3616.04 in a decreasing annuity on June 1, 1981. Beginning June 1, 1982 he was sent a check for $2000.00 per year for two years. The account paid 7% compounded annually. Complete the following decreasing annuity table for Fred's account.

Date	Principal	Interest	Balance Before Withdrawal	Withdrawal	Balance After Withdrawal
6/1/1981	$3616.04	–	$3616.04	–	$3616.04
6/1/1982	$3616.04	_____	_____	$2000.00	_____
6/1/1983	_____	_____	_____	$2000.00	_____

Note in Example 1 that Janice was able to draw $40,000.01 from the annuity even though her grandfather deposited only $36,298.95. The difference of $3701.06 represents the interest earned during the four years. The initial deposit of a decreasing annuity is called its **present value**, P. The formula for P is

$$P = W\left(\frac{n}{R}\right)\left[1 - \left(\frac{1}{1+\frac{R}{n}}\right)^{N}\right]$$

where

P = initial deposit (present value)

W = amount of each withdrawal

n = number of withdrawals *per year*

N = *total* number of withdrawals

R = annual percentage rate

      (compounded n times per year).

For a decreasing annuity, the first withdrawal does not occur until after one interest period has elapsed. For instance, in Example 1, the interest period is one year and the first withdrawal occurred one year after the initial deposit.

EXAMPLE 2   Finding the initial deposit for a decreasing annuity

Sharon and Tom King are planning to start their own business. During the first year, they expect minimal profits and they plan not to draw any personal income from the business until the second year. How much should Sharon and Tom set aside at the beginning of the year in a decreasing annuity paying $3\frac{1}{2}\%$ compounded monthly in order to withdraw $1000.00 per month for one year?

SOLUTION

For this exercise, we have $R = 0.035$, $W = \$1000.00$, $n = 12$, and $N = 12$. Therefore, the initial deposit should be

EXAMPLE 2

Steps	Display
0.035 [÷] 12 [=]	0.002916667
[+] 1 [=]	1.002916667
[1/x]	0.997091816
[y^x] 12 [=]	0.965654608
[+/−] [+] 1 [=]	0.034345392
[×] 12 [=]	0.412144704
[÷] 0.035 [=]	11.77556299
[×] 1000 [=]	11775.56299

$$P = W\left(\frac{n}{R}\right)\left[1 - \left(\frac{1}{1 + \frac{R}{n}}\right)^N\right]$$

$$= (\$1000.00)\left(\frac{12}{0.035}\right)\left[1 - \left(\frac{1}{1 + \frac{0.035}{12}}\right)^{12}\right]$$

$$\approx \$11,775.56.$$

Thus, Sharon and Tom should deposit \$11,775.56 in the annuity in order to draw \$12,000.00 over the period of one year. ◆

Try one!

Mark Blackwell is planning to take a year off of work to get his master's degree. In order to have enough money to live, he decides to set aside money in a decreasing annuity. How much should he put in an annuity paying 5% compounded monthly in order to withdraw \$1200.00 per month for one year?

Answer: ____________________

| EXAMPLE 3 | Finding the initial deposit for a decreasing annuity |

A particular community organization wishes to award five $10,000.00 scholarships per year (a total of $50,000.00 awarded per year) for the next 20 years to deserving students. How much should the organization have deposited in a decreasing annuity paying $7\frac{3}{4}\%$ compounded annually in order to pay for the scholarships?

SOLUTION

For this exercise, we have $R = 0.0775, W = \$50,000.00$, $n = 1$, and $N = 20$. Therefore, the initial deposit should be

$$P = W \left(\frac{n}{R}\right)\left[1 - \left(\frac{1}{1 + \dfrac{R}{n}}\right)^N\right]$$

$$= (\$50,000.00)\left(\frac{1}{0.0775}\right)\left[1 - \left(\frac{1}{1 + 0.0775}\right)^{20}\right]$$

$$\approx \$500,176.41. \qquad\qquad\qquad \blacklozenge$$

Example 3 demonstrates that by giving out a total of $1,000,000.00 in scholarships over the course of 20 years rather than all in the same year, the organization can save roughly half a million dollars!

Many people associate the word annuity with a retirement plan in which a person pays *into* an increasing annuity and then draws from the annuity after retirement. The federal government has passed legislation that allows taxpayers to set aside regular deposits in a **tax-deferred annuity program**. The three basic types of programs are called the **IRA** (individual retirement account), the **Keough plan** (for the self-employed, similar to an IRA), and the **401(k) plan** (named for the Internal Revenue Service code section in which its regulations are defined). The next example describes a typical situation.

EXAMPLE 4 **Combining an increasing annuity with a decreasing annuity**

Larry Sutton is self-employed and wishes to set up his own retirement plan through a savings and loan association. Larry is 30 years old and plans to retire at age 65. How much should he set aside in an increasing (tax-deferred) annuity paying 5% compounded monthly in order to withdraw $2500.00 per month for 20 years beginning at age 65?

SOLUTION

To begin, we need to determine the "initial deposit" Larry must have in his account at age 65 in order to draw $2500.00 per month for 20 years at 5% compounded monthly. For this we have $R = 0.05$, $W = \$2500.00$, $n = 12$, and $N = 20(12) = 240$. Thus, we have

$$P = W\left(\frac{n}{R}\right)\left[1 - \left(\frac{1}{1 + \frac{R}{n}}\right)^N\right]$$

$$= (\$2500.00)\left(\frac{12}{0.05}\right)\left[1 - \left(\frac{1}{1 + \frac{0.05}{12}}\right)^{240}\right]$$

$$\approx \$378,813.28.$$

Now, using the formula for increasing annuities in Section 3, we need to find how much Larry would need to deposit each month at 5% compounded monthly for 35 years in order to end up with a balance of $378,813.28. In this case we have $R = 0.05$, $n = 12$, $A = \$378,813.28$, and $N = 35(12) = 420$. Thus, Larry's monthly deposit over the 35 years should be

$$\text{Monthly Deposit} = \frac{A}{\left[\left(1 + \frac{R}{n}\right)^N - 1\right]\left(1 + \frac{n}{R}\right)} \quad \text{(from section 3)}$$

$$= \frac{\$378,813.28}{\left[\left(1 + \frac{0.05}{12}\right)^{420} - 1\right]\left(1 + \frac{12}{0.05}\right)} \approx \$332.05. \quad \blacklozenge$$

Try one!

Larry Sutton wants to set up a second retirement plan for his wife since she, too, is self-employed. She is 25 years old and plans to retire at age 60. How much should Larry set aside in an increasing (tax-deferred) annuity paying 5% compounded monthly in order to withdraw $1000.00 per month for 20 years beginning at age 60?

Answer: _____

Figure 1 graphically illustrates Larry's combination of a 35-year increasing annuity followed by a 20-year decreasing annuity.

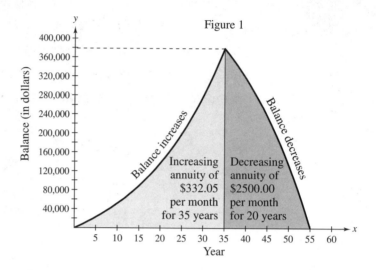

Figure 1

Table 9 gives some examples of increasing annuities followed by a 20-year decreasing annuity paying $1000.00 per month.

TABLE 9 — MONTHLY DEPOSIT FOR AN INCREASING ANNUITY THAT CONVERTS TO A DECREASING ANNUITY PAYING $1000.00 PER MONTH FOR 20 YEARS

Annual Percentage Rate	Monthly Deposit	Monthly Deposit	Monthly Deposit	Monthly Deposit	Monthly Deposit	Monthly Deposit	Monthly Deposit
	15 years	*20 years*	*25 years*	*30 years*	*35 years*	*40 years*	*45 years*
5%	$564.54	$367.11	$253.39	$181.31	$132.82	$98.88	$74.46
$5\frac{1}{2}\%$	$519.15	$332.19	$225.39	$158.39	$113.86	$83.12	$61.33
6%	$477.57	$300.59	$200.41	$138.26	$97.48	$69.74	$50.39
$6\frac{1}{2}\%$	$439.48	$272.02	$178.15	$120.60	$83.36	$58.42	$41.32
7%	$404.57	$246.17	$158.30	$105.11	$71.20	$48.85	$33.81
$7\frac{1}{2}\%$	$372.57	$222.78	$140.62	$91.55	$60.75	$40.80	$27.62
8%	$343.21	$201.63	$124.88	$79.69	$51.77	$34.02	$22.52
$8\frac{1}{2}\%$	$316.27	$182.49	$110.87	$69.32	$44.08	$28.33	$18.33
9%	$291.53	$165.17	$98.40	$60.26	$37.50	$23.57	$14.90

The formula for the initial deposit in a decreasing annuity can be altered to find the **amount of withdrawal** *W* for a given deposit as follows.

$$W = P\left[\frac{\frac{R}{n}}{1 - \left(\frac{1}{1 + \frac{R}{n}}\right)^N}\right]$$

where

P = initial deposit (present value)

W = amount of each withdrawal

n = number of withdrawals *per year*

N = *total* number of withdrawals

R = annual percentage rate

(compounded *n* times per year).

EXAMPLE 5   Finding the amount of each withdrawal in a decreasing annuity

Kathy Kraus received an inheritance from her grandmother's estate that amounted to $75,000.00 after taxes. Kathy deposited the money in a decreasing annuity that paid $4\frac{3}{4}\%$ compounded monthly. How much can Kathy withdraw each month over a period of **a.** ten years and **b.** 20 years?

a. For ten years, we have $P = \$75,000.00$, $R = 0.475$, $n = 12$, and $N = 10(12) = 120$. Thus, the amount of each withdrawal is

$$W = P\left[\frac{\frac{R}{n}}{1 - \left(\frac{1}{1 + \frac{R}{n}}\right)^N}\right]$$

$$= (\$75,000.00)\left[\frac{\frac{0.0475}{12}}{1 - \left(\frac{1}{1 + \frac{0.0475}{12}}\right)^{120}}\right]$$

$$\approx \$786.36.$$

Calculator Hints

$$W = P\left[\frac{\frac{R}{n}}{1 - \left(\frac{1}{1 + \frac{R}{n}}\right)^N}\right]$$

To find the amount of each withdrawal in a decreasing annuity using your calculator, apply the following steps:

1. Divide R by n and store the result.

2. Add 1 and press the $\boxed{1/x}$ key.

3. Raise to the *N*th power, change signs, and add 1.

4. Press the $\boxed{1/x}$ key

5. Multiply by memory.

6. Multiply by P.

7. Round to the nearest cent.

EXAMPLE 5a

Steps	Display
0.0475 $\boxed{\div}$ 12 $\boxed{=}$	0.003958333
$\boxed{STO}$	0.003958333
$\boxed{+}$ 1 $\boxed{=}$	1.003958333
$\boxed{1/x}$	0.996057273
$\boxed{y^x}$ 120 $\boxed{=}$	0.622468429
$\boxed{+/-}$ $\boxed{+}$ 1 $\boxed{=}$	0.377531571
$\boxed{1/x}$	2.648785098
$\boxed{\times}$ $\boxed{RCL}$ $\boxed{=}$	0.010484774
$\boxed{\times}$ 75,000 $\boxed{=}$	786.3580759

b. For 20 years, we have $P = \$75{,}000.00$, $R = 0.475$, $n = 12$, and $N = 20(12) = 240$. Thus, the amount of each withdrawal is

$$W = P\left[\dfrac{\dfrac{R}{n}}{1 - \left(\dfrac{1}{1 + \frac{R}{n}}\right)^{N}}\right]$$

$$= (\$75{,}000.00)\left[\dfrac{\dfrac{0.0475}{12}}{1 - \left(\dfrac{1}{1 + \frac{0.0475}{12}}\right)^{240}}\right]$$

$$\approx \$484.67. \qquad\qquad \blacklozenge$$

Try one!

How much can Kathy Kraus (from Example 5) withdraw per month over a period of 30 years?

Answer: _____

In Example 5 and its corresponding Try one!, note that the longer Kathy extends the withdrawal period of her decreasing annuity, the less she can withdraw each month. A less obvious observation is that the longer Kathy extends the annuity, the larger her total withdrawal will be. To see this, we multiply the number of withdrawals by the amount of each withdrawal to obtain the following.

For 10 years: total withdrawal = (120)($786.36) = $94,363.20

For 20 years: total withdrawal = (240)($484.67) = $116,320.80

For 30 years: total withdrawal = (360)($391.24) = $140,846.40

Important Terms

n, number of withdrawals per year

R, annual percentage rate

N, total number of withdrawals

W, amount of each withdrawal

decreasing annuity

Important Formulas

$$P = W\left(\frac{n}{R}\right)\left[1 - \left(\frac{1}{1 + \frac{R}{n}}\right)^N\right]$$

$$W = P\left[\frac{\frac{R}{n}}{1 - \left(\frac{1}{1 + \frac{R}{n}}\right)^N}\right]$$

CONSUMER HINTS

- If you qualify for an IRA, a Keough plan, or a 401(k) plan, shop around before deciding on a particular plan. Slight variations in interest rates can result in great differences in benefits. Remember that the sooner you enroll in such a plan, the more time your money will have to earn interest.

- If you are planning your retirement through an increasing annuity followed by a decreasing annuity, do not underestimate what you will need to maintain a comfortable living standard. You must consider that the cost of living changes over time and that the value of the dollar will most likely decline.

SECTION 3 EXERCISES

1. Carolyn North's father deposited $43,899.77 in a decreasing annuity on January 2, 1996. Carolyn planned to begin a five-year medical volunteer program in January 1997. At that time, Carolyn will begin drawing $10,000.00 per year for five years. Complete the following decreasing annuity table assuming the account pays $4\frac{1}{2}\%$ annually.

Date	Principal	Interest	Balance Before Withdrawal	Withdrawal	Balance After Withdrawal
1/2/1996	$43,899.77	–	$43,899.77	–	$43,899.77
1/2/1997	$43,899.77	_____	_____	$10,000.00	_____
1/2/1998	_____	_____	_____	$10,000.00	_____
1/2/1999	_____	_____	_____	$10,000.00	_____
1/2/2000	_____	_____	_____	$10,000.00	_____
1/2/2001	_____	_____	_____	$10,000.00	_____

2. Cathy Fisher is taking a six-month maternity leave and plans to withdraw $1000.00 per month beginning on April 1, 1997. The withdrawals will be made from a special account Cathy set up on March 1, 1997 with a deposit of $5887.88. Assuming that Cathy's account pays $6\frac{1}{2}\%$ compounded monthly, complete the following decreasing annuity table.

Date	Principal	Interest	Balance Before Withdrawal	Withdrawal	Balance After Withdrawal
3/1/1997	$5887.88	–	$5887.88	–	$5887.88
4/1/1997	$5887.88	_____	_____	$1000.00	_____
5/1/1997	_____	_____	_____	$1000.00	_____
6/1/1997	_____	_____	_____	$1000.00	_____
7/1/1997	_____	_____	_____	$1000.00	_____
8/1/1997	_____	_____	_____	$1000.00	_____
9/1/1997	_____	_____	_____	$1000.02	_____

3. Robert Simpson inherited a large sum of money from his grandparents' estate. Part of this inheritance was placed in a decreasing annuity that will pay Robert $2500.00 per month for 25 years. If the annuity pays 5% compounded monthly and the initial deposit was $427,650.09, complete the following table showing the first six withdrawals. Over the period of 25 years, how much will Robert withdraw from this account? (Assume the initial deposit was made on May 1, 1995.)

Date	Principal	Interest	Balance Before Withdrawal	Withdrawal	Balance After Withdrawal
5/1/1995	$427,650.09	–	$427,650.09	–	$427,650.09
6/1/1995	$427,650.09	_____	_____	$2500.00	_____
7/1/1995	_____	_____	_____	$2500.00	_____
8/1/1995	_____	_____	_____	$2500.00	_____
9/1/1995	_____	_____	_____	$2500.00	_____
10/1/1995	_____	_____	_____	$2500.00	_____
11/1/1995	_____	_____	_____	$2500.00	_____

Total Withdrawn: _____

In Exercises 4–7, find **a.** the initial deposit (present value), **b.** the total amount withdrawn, and **c.** the total interest.

4. A decreasing annuity paying $2000.00 per year for ten years at 4% compounded annually.

Initial Deposit: _____

Total Withdrawn: _____

Total Interest: _____

5. A decreasing annuity paying $500.00 per month for two years at $5\frac{1}{2}\%$ compounded monthly.

Initial Deposit: _____

Total Withdrawn: _____

Total Interest: _____

6. A decreasing annuity paying $5000.00 per quarter for 20 years at 10% compounded quarterly.

Initial Deposit: _____

Total Withdrawn: _____

Total Interest: _____

7. A decreasing annuity paying $10,000.00 per year for ten years at $3\frac{1}{4}$% compounded annually.

Initial Deposit: _____

Total Withdrawn: _____

Total Interest: _____

In Exercises 8–11, find the amount of each periodic withdrawal.

8. Yearly withdrawals from a $50,000.00 decreasing annuity at 4% compounded annually over a period of **a.** five years, **b.** ten years, **c.** 20 years.

Five Years: _____

Ten Years: _____

20 Years: _____

9. Monthly withdrawals from a $50,000.00 decreasing annuity at $7\frac{1}{2}\%$ compounded monthly over a period of **a.** five years, **b.** ten years, **c.** 20 years.

Five Years: _____

Ten Years: _____

20 Years: _____

10. Monthly withdrawals from a $100,000.00 decreasing annuity at $9\frac{1}{4}\%$ compounded monthly over a period of **a.** ten years, **b.** 20 years **c.** 30 years.

Ten Years: _____

20 Years _____

30 Years: _____

11. Quarterly withdrawals from a $10,000.00 decreasing annuity at 6% compounded quarterly over a period of **a.** two years, **b.** five years, **c.** ten years.

Two Years: _____

Five Years: _____

Ten Years: _____

Table 9 (page 96) gives the monthly deposit (in an increasing annuity) required to build a decreasing annuity paying $1000.00 per month for 20 years. In Exercises 12-15, find **a.** the monthly deposit, **b.** the total deposit, and **c.** the total interest earned by the time the account is closed.

12. Monthly deposits for 20 years at 7% compounded monthly.

Monthly Deposit: _____

Total Deposit: _____

Total Interest: _____

13. Monthly deposits for 15 years at $7\frac{1}{2}\%$ compounded monthly.

Monthly Deposit: _____

Total Deposit: _____

Total Interest: _____

14. Monthly deposits for 40 years at 5% compounded monthly.

Monthly Deposit: _____

Total Deposit: _____

Total Interest: _____

15. Monthly deposits for 30 years at $5\frac{1}{2}\%$ compounded monthly.

Monthly Deposit: _____

Total Deposit: _____

Total Interest: _____

16. David Spenser is self-employed and wishes to set up his own retirement plan. He is 35 years old and plans to retire at age 62. How much should he set aside in an increasing (tax deferred) annuity paying $4\frac{1}{2}\%$ compounded monthly in order to withdraw \$2000.00 per month for 25 years? (Assume that David has 27 full years in which to make payments.)

Answer: _____

17. Christine Sutton wishes to set up a retirement plan to supplement her social security retirement benefits. To do this, Christine makes monthly payments into an increasing annuity, which at age 62 will begin paying her \$1000.00 per month for 20 years. If the annuity pays $7\frac{3}{4}\%$ compounded monthly and Christine is 40 years old, how much should she set aside each month? (Assume that Christine has 22 full years in which to make payments.)

Answer: _____

18. Henry Thorpe has a $25,000.00 life insurance policy. Should Henry die, his wife Cora can elect to take the $25,000.00 in one payment or have equal monthly payments from the policy for 20 years. How much would Cora receive each month if she takes the second option? Assume that the insurance company pays $6\frac{1}{2}\%$ compounded monthly.

Answer: _____

Section 5
Spotlight On The Banker

Bankers are responsible for careful handling of money, dissemination of financial advice, promotion of the bank's products and services, and perhaps the most important responsibility of all is customer service. Whether you are a responsible high school student or have a doctorate in business administration, there is a position for you in the banking industry ranging from that of teller to branch manager or maybe even bank president!

The bank teller is probably the most visible employee in a bank. Customer service is therefore one of the most important jobs the teller performs. The teller handles the customer's deposits and withdrawals, provides a receipt to the customer for all transactions performed, and identifies whether or not the customer needs any further assistance. The teller is also responsible for recording all transactions in the bank's computerized database, keeping an accurate cash drawer, and balancing the cash drawer upon the conclusion of every shift.

To be a bank teller you need not have a college degree; however, the handling of a customer's money requires a great deal of trust. Most banks prefer that teller candidates have prior cash handling experience, a professional appearance, good customer service skills, and the ability to perform accurate data entry. Since tellers perform tasks ranging from debits, credits, and coin orders to currency exchange and issuance of bank checks, working as a teller is a great way to learn about the basic operations of a bank.

Full-time bank teller benefits may include medical insurance, paid vacations and holidays, vision and dental insurance and even employee tuition assistance programs which encourage educational advancement. As a teller without experience, you can earn about $6.50 per hour to start. As you gain experience this rate can increase to $10.00 or more per hour depending on your responsibilities, training, and location. Often a bank teller is trained to educate customers about the various types of accounts and financial services available. Tellers briefly explain these services and then refer interested customers to customer service managers, whose duties are discussed later in this section.

Some of the other positions in the bank that require a high school diploma include account executives, administrative assistants, customer service representatives and loan assistants, which, like the position of teller, are rewarding careers and may lead to promotion within the bank.

Positions in the bank requiring a college degree include accountants, loan officers, credit analysts, human resource administrators and managers. Branch and customer service managers are responsible for organization of all staff work, the promotion of products and services, and the development and implementation of sales strategies within the branch. Customer service managers sometimes assist in the opening of checking and savings accounts. They counsel customers about the various types of products and services and interview customers regarding their loans and investments. The bank's human resource manager is responsible for managing employee salaries and benefits, and does the hiring and training of new employees.

Financial managers make decisions in accordance with bank, state, and federal regulations. These managers are highly trained and are expected to have detailed knowledge of other related industries such as insurance, real estate, and securities. While a bachelors degree is all that is necessary for becoming a financial manager, most banks look favorably upon those who have obtained an MBA (masters of business administration). It is also important in today's complex global economy that financial managers participate in continuing education to keep up with the latest trends and regulations.

If you work for a large bank, you may have the opportunity to take part in a management training program. These larger banks feel it is important to train their own employees and like to promote from within. Salaries at the management level vary greatly by education, experience, location, and area of specialization, and benefits packages may include health and dental insurance, retirement plans and opportunities for education and advancement.

If you are interested in pursuing a career in banking, it is a good idea to talk to a friend or relative who is currently working in the industry. You can also go to your local bank and ask questions about the specific requirements for employment. Some banks offer internships to interested students so that they can determine if banking is an appropriate career choice. Keep in mind that while a college degree may be required for advancement to upper management, the most important qualifications for getting your foot in the door are a good academic record, honesty, responsiblity, integrity, professional appearance, and a dedication to customer and community service.

For more information on careers in banking, you can contact the following organizations.

American Bankers Association
1120 Connecticut Ave. NW
Washington, DC 20036

Bank Administration Institute
60 Gould Center
Rolling Meadows, IL 60008

Institute of Financial Education
111 East Wacker Dr., Suite 900
Chicago, IL 60601-4389

National Association of Bank Women
500 North Michigan Avenue, Suite 1400
Chicago, IL 60611

Independent Bankers Association of America
One Thomas Circle, NW
Washington, DC 20005

SECTION 5 EXERCISES

1. You are working as a bank teller and a regular customer, Mr. Burdick, asks you to tell him how much interest he earned on his passbook account last year. You access his account on the computer and find that his balance at the beginning of the year was $695.57, his balance at the end of the year was $723.39, and that he made no deposits and no withdrawals the whole year. How much interest did Mr. Burdick make during the year?

Answer: _____

Determine the annual percentage rate (simple interest) for Mr. Banks' account.

Answer: _____

2. As a customer service representative, you often get calls from customers about their bank statements. Mrs. Newberry called and said that some of the numbers on her annual passbook statement were hard to read. She told you that the balance at the beginning of the year was $1895.43 and that the only other number she could read was the interest earned during the year which was $71.08. Mrs. Newberry wants to verify the balance at the end of the year. How much does Mrs. Newberry have in her account at the end of the year if there were no deposits and no withdrawals made?

Answer: _____

Determine the annual percentage rate (simple interest) for Mrs. Newberry's account.

Answer: _____

3. On January 17, 1992 John Martin made a deposit of $1300.00 into a passbook savings account at 3% simple interest. Mr. Martin then closed the account on September 21 of the same year.

Find the number of days in the interest period.

Answer: _____

Find the amount of interest earned during this period.

Answer: _____

4. One of your customers, Mr. Stevens, is trying to decide which account is the best investment for his purpose. The passbook savings account offers 4% simple interest per year. The tax-free municipal bond offers only $3\frac{1}{4}\%$. If Mr. Stevens has $1200.00 to deposit and he is in a 25% tax bracket, which of the two savings plans would be the better investment?

Answer: _____

5. Kelly Williams has an account that she opened five years ago with $2500.00. The account has earned 5% interest compounded monthly for the entire five years. She has never deposited nor withdrawn any money. How much interest did Kelly earn during the five-year period?

Answer: _____

6. You are a customer service representative in a bank and a customer, Mrs. Snell, is trying to decide if she wants to open an account. She has already been to another bank and knows that she can get a five-year certificate of deposit in the amount of $10,000.00 that pays 4% compounded quarterly. You cannot offer her a better interest rate for her certificate, but you can offer her the benefit of continuous compounding. Mrs. Snell says that she needs to know exactly how much more she will get in your bank. Over the course of five years, how much more interest will Mrs. Snell earn with continuous compounding in your bank rather than at the other bank with quarterly compounding?

Answer: _____

7. Robert and Janis Crawford are trying to save as much as possible for their first home. They want to set aside $500.00 per month for the next four years in an annuity paying 6% compounded monthly. They approach you at the bank to find out how much they will have in the account at the end of the four years. How much will the Crawfords have for their downpayment at the end of the four years?

Answer: _____

8. A teenager named Jason comes into the bank and explains that he needs to save $1500.00 for an old car that he wants to fix up. The car belongs to a friend who can wait only one year before he needs the cash for college and has to sell it to someone else. How much should Jason set aside each week in an account that pays $5\frac{1}{2}$% compounded weekly in order to reach $1500.00 in one year? Assume Jason will get 52 paychecks during the year.

Answer: _____

9. A friend of yours comes to you since she knows you work in a bank and asks you how to set up an early retirement plan at your bank. She is self-employed and just got a large inheritance. She told you that she wants to withdraw $2000.00 per month for the next 25 years. You know that your bank has an annuity program offering 6% interest compounded monthly. How much do you tell her she would need to deposit in order to withdraw $2000.00 per month for the next 25 years?

Answer: _____

10. Mr. Winston, one of your regular bank customers, approaches you and wants to discuss his retirement. Even though his company offers a retirement plan, he wants to be sure to have enough money to do some travelling when he retires. He wants to have an additional $1000.00 per month for five years following his retirment at age 65. Mr. Winston is currently 40 years old and needs to know how much he should deposit per month into an annuity that pays 5% compounded monthly in order to withdraw the $1000.00 per month for five years. How much should Mr. Winston set aside per month until age 65? (Assume that he has a full 25 years in which to make payments.)

Answer: _____

Solutions to "Try one!" Exercises

SECTION 1

Page 2

$$I = A - P = \$2593.75 - \$2500.00 = \$93.75$$

Page 4

$$I = PRT = (1750.00)(0.05)(1) = \$87.50$$

Page 6

In this case we have $P = \$750.00$, $R = 0.0425$, and $D = 175$. So we have $I = PRT = PR\left(\frac{D}{365}\right) = (\$750.00)(0.0425)\left(\frac{175}{365}\right) \approx \$15.28$. And the balance after 175 days is $A = P + I = \$750.00 + \$15.28 = \$765.28$.

Page 8

Since the deposit was made after 3:00 p.m., the deposit will not be posted until the next working day which is Tuesday, December 26. (Monday is the Christmas holiday.)

Page 10

a. Since August 27, 1995 is day 239, $n = 239$. December 16, 1995 is day 350; therefore, $m = 350$. Using the formula $D = m - n$, we have $D = m - n = 350 - 239 = 111$ days.

b. Since February 11, 1996 is day 42, $n = 42$. January 7, 1997 is day 7; therefore, $m = 7$. Since 1996 is a leap year and the time period involves two calendar years, we use the formula $D = 366 + m - n$. So, we have $D = 366 + m - n = 366 + 7 - 42 = 331$ days.

Page 12

From January 19, 1996 to December 2, 1996 we have $D = 337 - 19 = 318$.

Since $P = \$968.50$, $I = \$28.39$ and 1996 is a leap year, we have

$$R = \frac{I}{P\left(\frac{D}{366}\right)} = \frac{\$28.39}{(\$968.50)\left(\frac{318}{366}\right)} \approx 0.0337 = 3.37\%.$$

Page 14

For the tax-exempt municipal bond, the annual effective yield is

$$Y = \frac{I}{P} = \frac{\$75.00}{\$2500.00} = 0.03 = 3\%.$$

Page 16

For a 30% tax bracket, we have $b = 0.30$ and

$$Y^* = \frac{(\$75.00)(1 - 0.30)}{\$2000.00} = 0.02625 \approx 2.63\%.$$

SECTION 2

Page 34

Quarter 1: $I = PRT = (\$1575.00)(0.035)(0.25) \approx \$13.78$

Balance $= \$1575.00 + \$13.78 = \$1588.78$

Quarter 2: $I = PRT = (\$1588.78)(0.035)(0.25) \approx \$13.90$

Balance $= \$1588.78 + \$13.90 = \$1602.68$

Quarter 3: $I = PRT = (\$1602.68)(0.035)(0.25) \approx \$14.02$

Balance $= \$1602.68 + \$14.02 = \$1616.70$

Quarter 4: $I = PRT = (\$1616.70)(0.035)(0.25) \approx \$14.15$

Balance $= \$1616.70 + \$14.15 = \$1630.85$

Page 35

First six months: $(\$2500.00)(0.0375)\left(\frac{1}{2}\right) \approx \$46.88$

Balance $= \$2500.00 + \$46.88 = \$2546.88$

Second six months: $(\$2546.88)(0.0375)\left(\frac{1}{2}\right) \approx \$47.75$

Balance $= \$2546.88 + \$47.75 = \$2594.63$

$$Y = \frac{I}{P} = \frac{\$2594.63 - \$2500.00}{\$2500.00} = \frac{\$94.63}{\$2500.00} \approx 0.037852 \approx 3.79\%$$

Page 38

One Year: $A = (\$1500.00)\left(1 + \frac{0.0425}{365}\right)^{365} \approx \$1565.12$

Four Years: $A = (\$1500.00)\left(1 + \frac{0.0425}{365}\right)^{1460} \approx \$1777.94$

$$Y = \frac{I}{P} = \frac{\$1565.12 - \$1500.00}{\$1500.00} = \frac{\$65.12}{\$1500.00} \approx 0.043413333 \approx 4.34\%$$

Page 41

One Year: $A = Pe^{RT} \approx (\$1500.00)e^{(0.0425)(1)} \approx \$1565.12$

Four Years: $A = Pe^{RT} \approx (\$1500.00)e^{(0.0425)(4)} \approx \$1777.96$

Page 45

a. From January 1 to April 4, Jason would earn $D = m - n = 94 - 1 = 93$ days' interest on a beginning balance of \$1075.50. So,

$$A = (\$1075.50)\left(1 + \frac{0.04}{365}\right)^{93} \approx \$1086.52.$$

After the \$350.00 deposit on April 4, his balance would be

$$A = \$1086.52 + \$350.00 = \$1436.52.$$

b. From April 4 to December 15, Jason's balance would grow to

$$A = (\$1436.52)\left(1 + \frac{0.04}{365}\right)^{349 - 94} \approx \$1477.23.$$

His \$300.00 withdrawal would leave Jason with a December 15 balance of

$$A = \$1477.23 - \$300.00 = \$1177.23.$$

Page 45 cont.

From December 15 to January 1, Jason's balance would grow to

$$A = (\$1177.23)\left(1 + \tfrac{0.04}{365}\right)^{365 + 1 - 349} \approx \$1179.43.$$

His total interest earned is

Interest $= \$1179.43 - \$1075.50 - \$350.00 + \$300 = \$53.93$.

Page 48

a. Quarter 1: $P = \$3000.00$, $I = PRT = (\$3000.00)(0.0375)\left(\tfrac{1}{4}\right) \approx \$28.13$,

balance $= \$3028.13$

Quarter 2: $P = \$3028.13$, $I = PRT = (\$3028.13)(0.0375)\left(\tfrac{1}{4}\right) \approx \$28.39$,

balance $= \$3056.52$

Quarter 3: $P = \$3056.52$, $I = PRT = (\$3056.52)(0.0375)\left(\tfrac{1}{4}\right) \approx \$28.65$,

balance $= \$3085.17$

Quarter 4: $P = \$3085.17$, $I = PRT = (\$3085.17)(0.0375)\left(\tfrac{1}{4}\right) \approx \$28.92$,

balance $= \$3114.09$

Penalty after nine months $= \$28.65 + \$28.39 = \$57.04$

b. Penalty after one year $= \$28.92 + \$28.65 = \$57.57$

$$Y = \frac{I}{P} = \frac{\$28.13 + \$28.39}{\$3000.00} = \frac{\$56.52}{\$3000.00} = 0.01884 \approx 1.88\%$$

SECTION 3

page 68

Deposit 1: Deposit $= \$100.00$, $I = PRT = (\$100.00)(0.035)\left(\tfrac{1}{4}\right) \approx \$0.88$,

balance $= \$100.88$

Deposit 2: Deposit = $100.00, $I = PRT = (\$200.88)(0.035)\left(\frac{1}{4}\right) \approx \$1.76$,

balance = $202.64

Deposit 3: Deposit = $100.00, $I = PRT = (\$302.64)(0.035)\left(\frac{1}{4}\right) \approx \$2.65$,

balance = $305.29

Deposit 4: Deposit = $100.00, $I = PRT = (\$405.29)(0.035)\left(\frac{1}{4}\right) \approx \$3.55$,

balance = $408.84

Total Interest = $8.84

page 70

a. $A = (\$100.00)\left[\left(1 + \frac{0.035}{12}\right)^{12} - 1\right]\left(1 + \frac{12}{0.035}\right) \approx \$1223.00$

b. $A = (\$100.00)\left[\left(1 + \frac{0.035}{12}\right)^{24} - 1\right]\left(1 + \frac{12}{0.035}\right) \approx \$2489.49$

page 72

$A = (\$2500.00)\left[\left(1 + 0.035\right)^{12} - 1\right]\left(1 + \frac{1}{0.035}\right) \approx \$38{,}418.92$

page 74

$A = (\$2000.00)\left[\left(1 + 0.0475\right)^{30} - 1\right]\left(1 + \frac{1}{0.0475}\right) \approx \$133{,}359.19$

page 76

Target Savings Plan: $(50)(\$25.00) + \$25.00 = \$1275.00$

Regular Bank Account:

$A = (\$25.00)\left[\left(1 + \frac{0.045}{52}\right)^{50} - 1\right]\left(1 + \frac{52}{0.045}\right) \approx \$1277.98$

Therefore, the regular bank account would have a higher final balance.

page 78

a. $P = \dfrac{\$25,000.00}{\left[\left(1 + \frac{0.045}{12}\right)^{84} - 1\right]\left(1 + \frac{12}{0.045}\right)} \approx \$252.81$

b. $P = \dfrac{\$25,000.00}{\left[\left(1 + \frac{0.06}{12}\right)^{84} - 1\right]\left(1 + \frac{12}{0.06}\right)} \approx \$239.02$

SECTION 4

page 90

June 1, 1982: $P = \$3616.04$, $I = PRT = (\$3616.04)(0.07)(1) \approx \$253.12$

Before $= P + I = \$3616.04 + \$253.12 = \$3869.16$

Withdrawal $= \$2000.00$

After $= \$3869.16 - \$2000.00 = \$1869.16$.

June 1, 1983: $P = \$1869.16$, $I = PRT = (\$1869.16)(0.07)(1) \approx \$130.84$

Before $= P + I = \$1869.16 + \$130.84 = \$2000.00$

Withdrawal $= \$2000.00$

After $= \$2000.00 - \$2000.00 = \$0.00$.

page 92

$$P = (\$1200.00)\left(\frac{12}{0.05}\right)\left[1 - \left(\frac{1}{1 + \frac{0.05}{12}}\right)^{12}\right]$$

$\approx \$14,017.47$

page 95

$R = 0.05$, $W = \$1000.00$, $n = 12$, and $N = 20(12) = 240$

$$P = (\$1000.00)\left(\frac{12}{0.05}\right)\left[1 - \left(\frac{1}{1 + \frac{0.05}{12}}\right)^{240}\right]$$

$\approx \$151,525.31$

page 95 cont.

$R = 0.05$, $n = 12$, $A = \$151{,}525.31$, and $N = 35(12) = 420$

$$\text{Monthly deposit} = \frac{\$151{,}525.31}{\left[\left(1 + \frac{0.05}{12}\right)^{420} - 1\right]\left(1 + \frac{12}{0.05}\right)} \approx \$132.82$$

page 98

$$W = (\$75{,}000.00)\left[\frac{\frac{0.0475}{12}}{1 - \left(\frac{1}{1 + \frac{0.0475}{12}}\right)^{360}}\right]$$

$$\approx \$391.24$$

Answers to Odd-Numbered Exercises

SECTION 1

1. a. $15.47 **b.** $52.06 **c.** $427.71   **3. a.** $18.29 **b.** $53.09 **c.** $23.87

5. $2.47   **7.** $4.75

9. $29.08   **11.** $7.40

13. $2.46   **15.** $4.73

17. $29.00   **19.** $7.38

21. 40 days   **23.** 66 days

25. $4.89   **27.** $5.42

29. 6.25%   **31.** 3.75%

33. 6.25%   **35.** 3.76%

37. 4.4%   **39.** 4.71%

41. 3.08%   **43.** 3.30%

45. a. $986.62 **b.** $5783.13

SECTION 2

1. Quarter 1: $P = \$500.00$, $I = \$3.75$, Balance = $503.75

   Quarter 2: $P = \$503.75$, $I \approx \$3.78$, Balance = $507.53

   Quarter 3: $P = \$507.53$, $I \approx \$3.81$, Balance = $511.34

   Quarter 4: $P = \$511.34$, $I \approx \$3.84$, Balance = $515.18

   $Y \approx 3.04\%$

3. Quarter 1: $P = \$5000.00$, $I = \$75.00$, Balance = $5075.00

   Quarter 2: $P = \$5075.00$, $I \approx \$76.13$, Balance = $5151.13

   Quarter 3: $P = \$5151.13$, $I \approx \$77.27$, Balance = $5228.40

   Quarter 4: $P = \$5228.40$, $I \approx \$78.43$, Balance = $5306.83

   $Y \approx 6.14\%$

5. Annually: $A = \$515.00$, $Y = 3.00\%$

Quarterly: $A \approx \$515.17$, $Y \approx 3.03\%$

Monthly: $A \approx \$515.21$, $Y \approx 3.04\%$

Daily: $A \approx \$515.23$, $Y \approx 3.05\%$

Continuously: $A \approx \$515.23$, $Y \approx 3.05\%$

7. Annually: $A = \$5300.00$, $Y = 6.00\%$

Quarterly: $A \approx \$5306.82$, $Y \approx 6.14\%$

Monthly: $A \approx \$5308.39$, $Y \approx 6.17\%$

Daily: $A \approx \$5309.16$, $Y \approx 6.18\%$

Continuously: $A \approx \$5309.18$, $Y \approx 6.18\%$

9. Annually: $A = \$333.91$ Quarterly: $A \approx \$334.63$

Monthly: $A \approx \$334.80$ Daily: $A \approx \$334.88$

Continuously: $A \approx \$334.88$

11. Annually: $A = \$15,529.69$ Quarterly: $A \approx \$15,643.77$

Monthly: $A \approx \$15,669.93$ Daily: $A \approx \$15,682.69$

Continuously: $A \approx \$15,683.12$

13. Annually: $A = \$30,054.35$ Quarterly: $A \approx \$30,609.31$

Monthly: $A \approx \$334.80$ Daily: $A \approx \$334.88$

Continuously: $A \approx \$334.88$

15. $3228.28   **17.** $610.70

19.

Date	Withdrawal	Deposit	Interest	Balance
Jan 1				$3162.47
Feb 16		$422.50	$24.00	$3608.97
July 14	$1250.00		$88.87	$2447.84
Aug 28		$150.00	$18.17	$2616.01
Jan 1			$54.74	$2670.75

Total Interest = $185.78

21. 2 years, 9 months: $A \approx \$1147.07$ **23.** $3351.67

3 years: $A \approx \$1161.47$

penalty: $14.40

25. a. After 93 months, the amount has doubled.

b. After 147 months, the amount has tripled.

SECTION 3

1. Deposit 1: Deposit = $1000.00, Principal = $1000.00
I = $50.00, Balance = $1050.00

Deposit 2: Deposit = $1000.00, Principal = $2050.00
I = $102.50, Balance = $2152.50

Deposit 3: Deposit = $1000.00, Principal = $3152.50
$I \approx$ $157.63, Balance = $3310.13

Deposit 4: Deposit = $1000.00, Principal = $4310.13
$I \approx$ $215.51, Balance = $4525.64

Deposit 5: Deposit = $1000.00, Principal = $5525.64
$I \approx$ $276.28, Balance = $5801.92

3. Deposit 1: Deposit = $500.00, Principal = $500.00
I = $15.00, Balance = $515.00

Deposit 2: Deposit = $500.00, Principal = $1015.00
I = $30.45, Balance = $1045.45

Deposit 3: Deposit = $500.00, Principal = $1545.45
$I \approx$ $46.36, Balance = $1591.81

Deposit 4: Deposit = $500.00, Principal = $2091.81
$I \approx$ $62.75, Balance = $2154.56

Deposit 5: Deposit = $500.00, Principal = $2654.56
$I \approx$ $79.64, Balance = $2734.20

Deposit 6: Deposit = $500.00, Principal = $3234.20
$I \approx$ $97.03, Balance = $3331.23

Deposit 7: Deposit = $500.00, Principal = $3831.23
$I \approx$ $114.94, Balance = $3946.17

Deposit 8: Deposit = $500.00, Principal = $4446.17
$I \approx$ $133.39, Balance = $4579.56

Deposit 9: Deposit = $500.00, Principal = $5079.56
$I \approx$ $152.39, Balance = $5231.95

Deposit 10: Deposit = $500.00, Principal = $5731.95
$I \approx$ $171.96, Balance = $5903.91

5. $A \approx$ $83,506.56   **7.** $A \approx$ $12,134.33   **9.** $A \approx$ $11,690.91

5. $A \approx \$83,506.56$ **7.** $A \approx \$12,134.33$ **9.** $A \approx \$11,690.91$

11. After four years: $A \approx \$11,106.26$

After six more years: $A \approx \$16,882.69$

13. $P \approx \$370.93$ **15. a.** $P \approx \$18.89$ **b.** $A \approx \$1221.39$

SECTION 4

1. January 2, 1993

$P = \$43,899.77, I \approx \$1975.49,$ before $= \$45,875.26$

withdrawal $= \$10,000.00,$ after $= \$35,875.26$

January 2, 1994

$P = \$35,875.26, I \approx \$1614.39,$ before $= \$37,489.65$

withdrawal $= \$10,000.00,$ after $= \$27,489.65$

January 2, 1995

$P = \$27,489.64, I \approx \$1237.03,$ before $= \$28,726.68$

withdrawal $= \$10,000.00,$ after $= \$18,726.68$

January 2, 1996

$P = \$18,726.68, I \approx \$842.70,$ before $= \$19,569.38$

withdrawal $= \$10,000.00,$ after $= \$9569.38$

January 2, 1997

$P = \$9569.38, I \approx \$430.62,$ before $= \$10,000.00$

withdrawal $= \$10,000.00,$ after $= \$27,489.65$

3. June 1, 1995

$P = \$427,650.09, I \approx \$1781.88,$ before $= \$429,431.97$

withdrawal $= \$2500.00,$ after $= \$426,931.97$

July 1,1995

$P = \$426,931.97, I \approx \$1778.88$, before $= \$428,710.85$

withdrawal $= \$2500.00$, after $= \$426,210.85$

August 1,1995

$P = \$426,210.85, I \approx \$1775.88$, before $= \$427,986.73$

withdrawal $= \$2500.00$, after $= \$425,486.73$

September 1,1995

$P = \$425,486.73, I \approx \$1772.86$, before $= \$427,259.59$

withdrawal $= \$2500.00$, after $= \$424,759.59$

October 1,1995

$P = \$424,759.59\ I \approx \$1769.83$, before $= \$426,529.42$

withdrawal $= \$2500.00$, after $= \$424,029.42$

November 1,1995

$P = \$424,029.42\ I \approx \$1766.79$, before $= \$425,796.21$

withdrawal $= \$2500.00$, after $= \$423,296.21$

Total withdrawn after 25 years: $750,000.00

5. a. $P \approx \$11,338.99$ **b.** $\$12,000.00$ **c.** $I = \$661.01$

7. a. $P \approx \$84,223.95$ **b.** $\$100,000.00$ **c.** $I = \$15,776.05$

9. a. $W \approx \$1001.90$ **b.** $W \approx \$593.51$ **c.** $\approx \$402.80$

11. a. $W \approx \$1335.84$ **b.** $W \approx \$582.46$ **c.** $W \approx \$334.27$

13. a. $\$372.57$ **b.** $\$67,062.60$ **c.** $\$172,937.40$

15. a. $\$158.39$ **b.** $\$57,020.40$ **c.** $\$182,979.60$

17. $P = \$121,810.31$, monthly deposit $= \$174.81$

SECTION 5

1. $I = \$27.82$ $R \approx 0.039995975 \approx 4.00\%$

3. $D = 248$ days (1992 is a leap year), $I \approx \$26.43$

5. $A \approx \$3208.40$

7. $A \approx \$27,184.16$

9. $P \approx \$310,413.73$